Errant Journeys

Errant Journeys

Adventure Travel in a Modern Age

David Zurick

Original drawings by Keith Otterson
Maps by Tim Krasnansky

 University of Texas Press, Austin

'95

First edition, 1995

Requests for permission to reproduce material from this work should be
sent to Permissions, University of Texas Press, Box 7819, Austin, TX
78713-7819.

∞ The paper used in this publication meets the minimum requirements
of American National Standard for Information Sciences—Permanence
of Paper for Printed Library Materials, ANSI Z39.48-1984.

LIBRARY OF CONGRESS CATALOGING-IN-PUBLICATION DATA

Zurick, David.
Errant journeys : adventure travel in a modern age / by David Zurick ;
original drawings by Keith Otterson ; maps by Tim Krasnansky.
        p.   cm.
    Includes index.
    ISBN 0-292-79805-9. — ISBN 0-292-79806-7 (pbk.)
    I. Ecotourism.   Title.
G155.A1Z87   1995
338.4'791—dc20   94-30763

Cecil Rajendra's poem "When the Tourists Flew In," from *Contours* 1,
No. 4 (3rd Quarter 1983): 9, is quoted by permission of *Contours*.

For Kilali

errant *adj.* 1. Roving, esp. in search of adventure.
        2. Straying from a proper course or standard;
        erring.

journey *n.* Travel from one place to another; a trip.

—*The American Heritage Dictionary of the English Language*

Contents

Acknowledgments

Although written in a year at my home in the Kentucky foothills, the work of this book spans decades and continents. Along the way, I have become indebted to so many people, so many *kinds* of persons, that it becomes impossible to name all those who contributed significantly to the completion of this work. Many of them lead quiet lives in remote places and will not even know of the existence of this book. Several persons, though, shine through the list and deserve special mention.

Craig Overly joined me in 1975 on my first tour of the world and has been a regular companion since those early days. My parents, Norman and Catherine, and the rest of my family have steadfastly watched me come and go, supporting me over the years with confidence that I would one day parlay my carefree journeys into a career. Nowadays, I travel with my wife, Kilali Alailima, who helps me to see the world with continually fresh eyes.

I wish to thank anthropologist Tom Fricke for his critical insights, humor, and good sense. Many other scholars have helped to shape this book directly and through their writings. Among them, I wish especially to thank Rich Schein for his review of the early stages of the manuscript. I have benefited from the support of the Department of Geography and Planning at Eastern Kentucky University, where I now teach and write. Numerous organizations have provided funding for various periods of geographical fieldwork, during which I also collected impressions and ideas that eventually went into the writing of this book. They include the National Science Foundation, O le Siosiomaga Society in Western Samoa, the East-West Center in Honolulu, Eastern Kentucky University, and the Kentucky Council for International Education.

I
Tourist
Trails

On a weathered signboard tacked to a scrub of juniper at the outskirts of a mountain village in Nepal, I read the words scrawled in English, "HERE IS COME MANY PEOPLES." Hewn neatly into the wood beneath appears the cursive Tibetan writing "OM," the meditative breath chanted by the monks who live in a nearby Buddhist monastery. The signboard marks the meeting of worlds; the Tibetan word encompasses a history that spans generations and anchors the place in a local tradition, but the English phrase obviously is intended for newcomers who visit this remote spot. It encompasses a new *geography* that links this place with the "outside" world. But who "is come" to this village, and why? Tucked into the sweep of the central Himalaya, accessible only by walking for a week or more over snowy passes, on steep trails that skirt gorges and avalanches, a place of strange customs, devoid of the sort of amenities that most tourists expect, it seemed an unlikely spot for foreigners. Yet, as I lingered for several days in the village, I met travelers from all over the world; some of them sported the bright Gore-Tex wear of holiday-makers, others donned the faded garb of the long-term Asian experience; all, however, wore the pained looks of discovery as they trekked on to more distant places within the encompassing mountains. Their visages showed both the physical stress of fatigue and the anxiety of as yet unfulfilled dreams. The more of them I saw, so much like myself, the greater became my own unrest and urge to move.

The tourists I met in that remote village along Nepal's northern border comprise a small and fairly adventurous group, but they join ranks with a quarter million other Westerners who visit the tiny mountainous country each year, and with several million more adventure travelers who journey annually from Europe and North America to explore what they consider to be some of the world's most exotic places. Over the years I've come to know many of them. We've met in the medinas of northern Africa and among the covered bazaars of central Asia, shared shepherds' huts and pots of salty tea high in the Himalaya, wandered together through ancient ruins in central Thailand and Central America, kayaked along empty Pacific beaches, and joined the throngs that weave crazily through the maddening streets of Third World cities. Along the way of such journeys ordinary things can seem magical and the landscapes of the imagination become real. Inner and outward travel may fuse in a gradual awakening of the senses and the ability to make sense out of them. But fragile and exotic destinations along the traveler's way are exposed, places that break easily under the influence of tourism's force, like thin panes of summer glass before a strong northern wind. Ironically, adventure tourism carries with it the very defilements that such tourists wish to escape, and their travel extends them to some of the world's most remote landscapes. Unwitting bearers of the worlds they have temporarily abandoned, adventure travelers unravel Western ways along the new tourist routes, where they connect with much older wefts of life to weave a fabric of change that covers with new patterns and textures the places that lie at the very edges of the world.

The changes that conventional tourism brings to the places where it occurs alarm those who believe them to be primarily negative. The critics of tourism argue that its economic benefits may not in the end outweigh its social and environmental costs. Such costs, borne primarily by the people and places tourists visit, may include widespread transformations of the natural landscape and equally pervasive shifts in the attitudes of host cultures. The tourism theme parks in the host countries are obvious examples of the extremes of such changes. In these places the built environment may have no relation to the world it is intended to portray, representing instead a myth manufactured by the travel industry to meet the tourists' expectations, and the people who inhabit them portray caricatures of themselves. More common perhaps, but initially less noticeable, are the subtle shifts endlessly reproduced in places around the world frequented by tourists—what were once social exchanges are now economic transactions, sacred rituals change to secular ceremonies, native dress becomes curio costumes, and the material trappings of the Western world assume the commonplace. The power of tourism in a place devoted to it is both frightening and seductive. It can transform places into theater, with events becoming drama and people becoming actors. In a slow, inexorable way, such places distance themselves from their commonness, that which holds their life but not the show that lures the tourists with their money.

High-volume mass tourism imparts the obvious consequences that the critics fear.[1] A less-known alternative type of tourism focuses on adventurous travel to the world's remote places. This is not large-scale tourism of the kind envisioned by the critics of conventional tourism; adventure travel may not produce the types of economic and social shifts that characterize full-blown mass tourism, but its impacts on those places where it occurs nonetheless can be considerable. I write as someone who in the past commonly avoided tourists but regularly sought out the adventurous travelers. I still do, but this division now strikes me as curious, and the distinction is less obvious to me now than it once was. While I have always intuitively seen my own travels as "alternative," only recently have I questioned the outcome of my past journeys for those places that lie in the wake of my path. How do the alternative tourists, often traveling singly, in pairs, or in small groups, change the places they visit? The question also concerns some tourism scholars. The geographer Richard Butler proposed the idea that just because alternative tourism is not "mass" tourism does not automatically mean that it carries no adverse consequences, that somehow it is a more *appropriate* form of tourism. He states that the often synonymous use of the terms *alternative* and *appropriate* is misleading, since it assumes only positive outcomes for the former. In fact, as Butler contends, scholars and tourism planners know too little about alternative tourism's long-term consequences to make such simplistic assertions.[2]

The scholars who study tourism seek objective explanations for what are essentially subjective experiences. Since there is no single experience, there can be no simple explanation. This is true for the tourists and for the places that host them. Tourists themselves and the visions and the changes that they carry with them may, in the end, provide the best insight into the meanings of travel. On many occasions, I've encountered groups of Westerners on guided tours in non-Western countries and wondered how each could achieve a personal immersion into the places they visit, when their time is structured, their exchanges buffered by the group, and their understandings filtered through the explanations of the guides. Yet, for each, it remains a solitary experience. But what must it mean for the places and the people such groups of tourists encounter, for them to meet not individuals but a parade of sightseers seemingly on a mission? And is it different for the adventurous tourists who travel alone, eschewing the well-worn routes and destinations in order to secure a more "exotic" or "authentic" experience?

In India there exists, as in another's dream or as a mirage, the fortress town of Jaisalmir, located on a low ridge amidst the shifting dunes of the western Rajasthan desert. Jaisalmir is a place as pretty as its name. The ornate structures of the town, ornamented with latticed balconies and secret interior courtyards, and made of huge carved sandstone blocks, line cobblestone streets polished from centuries of sandaled feet, and so narrow that the shadows of the adjoining houses darken them at midday and keep them cool. Steep conical rooftops with arabesque façades soar skyward to mark the Jain temples that punctuate the desert skyline. Hawkers come and go in the streets, announcing their wares in nasal, sing-song voices. Cattle lumber along twisted lanes and children scamper through the village square and among the crumbling walls of the older sections of town. Officious-looking clerks sitting cross-legged on pillows tend ledgers in the cloth shops, always with one eye to the moving panorama outside.

The town is a freeze-frame from mythical time. Water is drawn in wooden buckets from deep wells and hauled in clay vessels on the heads of robed women; merchants in flowing robes and upturned silken slippers sell jewelry and brocade cloth under bougainvillea sweeps; outside the town gates, camels balk when the heavy loads that they must carry across the desert stretches are placed on their sloping backs; from a distance, at sunset, the town's silhouette shows against the horizon as an image of a thousand nights. But now into the scene come increasing numbers of adventure travelers. Jaisalmir has become the terminus for a narrow-gauge railway that brings thousands of tourists each year to join the camel treks to more distant desert encampments. The town is a staging post for the new commercial journeys, just as it always has been a gateway to the desert trading routes. Safaris that once carried precious stones, incense, and contraband, now transport tourists, a new kind of gold. Where simple caravansaries once hosted scores of desert traders, courtyard inns now lodge tourists in relative comfort. In Jaisalmir, as in many such places, the anticipated prospects that tourism brings to the future economy dispel the many recollections of the past. The magic carpet dreams of the tourists meet the market dreams of Jaisalmir's entrepreneurs in a fantasy place that happens to be real. The impact that tourists have on this delicate place is first noticeable in a material way—restaurant and inn signs, tourist prices in the marketplaces, advertisements for camel safaris mark Jaisalmir's tourism landscape. Less obvious but more long-lasting consequences require a deeper look, for they strike at the very core of Jaisalmir's hidden society. The shifts it produces in the local economy and the wider perspective it requires of international finances reshape the contours of change in this ethereal place and others much like it. To understand these new patterns and what they imply for the futures of distant places requires some knowledge of how tourism works.

A New Wave of Travelers

Scholars, attempting to distinguish between various types of travelers, note different kinds of tourism. A common category is "mass" or conventional tourism, where the main purpose of the visitors is to enjoy leisure time in a new setting. Entire worlds have been created to accommodate this form of tourism, complete with theme parks and thematic experiences, lavish services, and a list of organized activities to schedule the day. If such tourists learn anything about the places they visit, it may be merely coincidental and not central to the experience. Even the resort surroundings give no clue into the wider world outside but are intended instead to make visitors "feel at home" in their foreign but luxurious settings. The tourist enclaves located along many tropical coastlines exemplify such places. They provide all manner of amenities, from teatime to tennis, to the point that tourists find it unnecessary to venture outside the manicured grounds. Occasionally, however, and for a costly sum, the resorts will organize group excursions to the outlying points of interest.

One sunny morning in Thailand, I observed such a group of Japanese tourists from my small thatch bungalow on one of the country's southern islands. A large bus deposited fifty or more of them on my beach. The tour leader, dressed in checkered slacks and white polo shirt, led the group to the water's edge where they all shed their outer clothing amidst laughter and clicking cameras. At a whistle sound, they entered the water together, stumbling over the knee-high waves and each other. After five minutes the whistle again blew and everyone immediately climbed out of the surf. They toweled off in unison, bought some trinkets that the local women were selling, and with yet another whistle boarded the bus and were speedily gone. The regimented visit lasted fifteen minutes, and I felt that my beach had been violated forever. I was wrong of course; it was not my beach, and in a matter of minutes the waves were again lulling me in my morning of leisure. The local vendors told me later that such excursions occur daily and that that was why they were on the beach with their tourist trade. I left wondering if the Japanese group's entire day was similar to that brief episode; I suspect that it was.

In contrast to those tourists found at the conventional resort destinations and on the guided tours conducted by the mainstream travel industry—people commonly referred to as conventional or "mass" tourists—passengers on the various types of "alternative" tours participate in new forms of global tourism. Distinguishing among the members of this latter group is made difficult by the dissembling array of labels that they have been given by the tourism industry and by those who study tourism. Perhaps the most basic distinction is that between tourist and traveler, although this, too, is not always clear. *The American Heritage Dictionary* defines a *tourist* simply as "A person who is traveling for pleasure," but it describes the term *travel*, and by extension, *traveler*, to mean "To go from one place to another," "A series of journeys," and "To toil." The former implies people who are interested primarily in recreation at the end of the journey, while the latter focus on the act of travel—where the journey, itself, and not its end is the paramount experience. A more comprehensive view of the meaning of *traveler* is shown in *Roget's Thesaurus*, which lists as synonyms for *traveler*: wayfarer, itinerant, adventurer, nomad, wanderer, rambler, gypsy, vagabond. Against the rather straightforward divide between *tourist* and *traveler* are the various confusing appellations given to both by the travel industry, the media, and the tourists themselves. It is a confounding glossary of somewhat arbitrary words. Frequently encountered phrases, fashionable buzzwords, include *ecotourism* or *nature tourism, ethnic* or *cultural tourism, mass tourism* and *appropriate tourism.* I will first attempt to define these terms and then introduce an additional one, *adventure travel,* which becomes the focus for much of this book.

Hector Caballos-Lascuria initially coined the term *ecotourist,* and in a recent international symposium on the subject held in Miami, he defined ecotourism as

. . . that segment of tourism that involves traveling to relatively undisturbed or uncontaminated natural areas with the
specific object of admiring, studying, and enjoying the scenery and its wild plants and animals, as well as any existing
cultural features (both past and present) found in these areas.
Ecotourism implies a scientific, esthetic, or philosophical approach, although the ecotourist is, of course, not required to
be a professional scientist, artist or philosopher. The main
point here is that the person that practices ecotourism has the
opportunity of immersing himself or herself in Nature in a
way that most people cannot enjoy in their routine, urban ex-
istences. This person will eventually acquire an awareness and
knowledge of the natural environment, together with its cultural aspects, that will convert him or her into somebody
keenly involved in conservation issues.[3]

I quote Caballos-Lascuria at length for two reasons. His definition, which is widely accepted within the emerging ecotravel industry, suggests a focus on the "pristine" world but prescribes no clear strategy for going about it. Simply defining a new geographic stage for tourism does not necessarily constitute a new *type* of tourism. Second, it suggests that participant "conversion" to conservation is an explicit goal of this form of tourism. The experiences of many host countries that encourage their visitors to engage in *eco*tourism suggest that the "eco" in ecotourism most often identifies *eco*nomics and not the *eco*logy that it invariably implies. The same Miami Symposium uncovered a wide range of definitions and views on ecotourism: it is "based *principally* on natural . . . resources"; it "differs from mass tourism based upon man-created attractions"; it "may include affluent individuals traveling to remote locations in high comfort"; and "ecotourism is an ambiguous term at best."[4] Sometimes, the phrase *nature tourism* replaces ecotourism, but the intention remains the same—to identify, design, and manage a natural resource–based tourism program that maximizes the economic benefit for local people while minimizing environmental impacts.[5] The fact that more tourists are looking for the alternative experiences provided by ecotourism is registered in its growing popularity (nature tourism now commands 10 percent of the U.S. travel industry) and in the recent deluge of international symposia, special publications, and new organizations centered on it.[6]

A second variant of alternative tourism is ethnic or cultural tourism. This often is subsumed under ecotourism because it includes not only nature-based tourism but also the indigenous cultures which may reside in the natural areas. The fact that ecotourism and ethnic tourism are interchanged suggests additional ambiguity in their conception and management. In fact, when tourism occurs in those natural areas that include a human component, the human systems are considered every bit as interesting as the natural systems. In addition to those ecotours that blend natural and cultural histories, the explicitly cultural tours focus only on human populations. The telling tale is that cultural or "ethnic" tourism is restricted to non-white, non-Western societies that hold some kind of special wonder for the essentially white and Western tourists—as if steelworkers in an industrial city were any less fascinating than hunter-gatherers in a tropical rain forest.

The designation of ecotourism and ethnic tourism results in what is described in the tourism industry generically as "alternative tourism." It implies a more sustainable, benign, and equitable form of travel that contrasts rather sharply with the consumptive, attraction-based mass tourism most commonly encountered at the established resort destinations. While it often is argued that differences do exist between the two in terms of their design, the type of involvement they require of the tourists, and their industrial management, the primary distinction between alternative and mass tourism appears to be geographic. The latter leads to the established resorts, while the former occurs precisely in those places where the others do not. Therefore, alternative tourism probably is not *alternative* to anything. The study of tourism and the sanguine welcome it receives among economic developers have failed to adequately distinguish among the various types of both mass and alternative tourism.

In the opinion of tourism scholar Linda Richter, the dialogue must move "beyond the decrying of mass travel or the extolling of particular alternatives toward a more complicated but hopefully more relevant concern with *appropriate* tourism."[7] Situated within this semantic conundrum is the idea of adventure travel, which is generally considered to be a variant of alternative tourism. World congresses have been held on the subject and the Adventure Travel Society was established recently as a trade association to address the planning and development issues of adventure tourism. I use the term here broadly to identify travel patterns that take Western people into what are essentially non-Western, geographically re-mote places. In general, such spots are already inhabited, so that adventure travel includes both the natural and cultural systems of the visited place. Moreover, adventure travel usually is linked to some thematic form of travel—safaris, trekking, kayaking, and in many cases simply local public transportation—which can be adventure enough for those coming from the industrial, conve-nience-oriented societies of the Western world. In any case, adventure travel has been with us for a very long time. It links back to the early explorers and to their circuitous paths of discovery. But it also forges entirely new opportunities for travel that are designed by the adventure tourism industry. The explicit use of the term *travel* by the tourism industry, rather than *tourism*, suggests the division between traveler and tourist proposed before. Adventurers in the near past most neatly fit the former, but modern adventure travel, with its highly developed itineraries, appears geared to a more conventional tourist, despite the adventure travel industry's proclamations to the contrary:

> We try to craft our trips with a watchmaker's care. But for the machinery to run well there has to be a motive force, a vision. This is especially true for a company like ours, which has stayed out of the mass market of tourism. Our vision grows out of the allure of magic places like Lhasa, Samarkand, Istanbul, Kathmandu, and Hunza.[8]

Adventure travel, as a new form of international tourism, began when Leo Le Bon and Mountain Travel first offered adventure tours for North Americans in the 1960s. Since then, the number of specialist adventure agencies in the United States alone has grown to over three hundred. Many hundreds more are located in the societies of Europe, Australia, and New Zealand, as well as in the destination countries themselves, where they aspire to be the harbingers of economic change and, ironically, modernity. Most of the Western agencies design itineraries that take tourists to the developing regions of the world, where they are found "bushwhacking through steaming jungles, riding camels across blazing deserts and climbing the flanks of glacier-clad peaks."[9] Such adventurers carry with them some of the behaviors and impacts of mass tourism, but they also contribute the new components of alternative tourism. In later chapters I talk about this as I describe old and new travel routes and destinations.

Because the alternative forms of tourism described here are smaller in scale than mass tourism, they involve fewer people and fewer conveniences. And because the places that alternative travelers visit are less traveled and require more innovative means of entry, the impacts of mass and alternative tourism will differ. These differences can be used by tourism planners to design alternative goals and means of travel. On the face of it, and maybe only because at present the numbers remain relatively small against tourism as a whole, adventure travel and the other forms of alternative tourism contrast with mass tourism in terms both of quantity and quality of experiences. But the subtle shifts in life's many routines and patterns that occur with the advance of adventure tourists into previously closed spaces become nonetheless noteworthy when measured against their absence, and they probably indicate more pronounced changes to come in the near future. These thoughts, however, are not paramount in the minds of all adventure tourists or those hosting them, not even when events forecast their occurrence.

One evening several years ago in a remote spot in the central Himalaya, exhausted after a full day of walking, my companions and I stopped for the night in a small, nondescript lodge located alongside the trail. It was quite cold, and after arranging our beds we found a place near the fire to sit, drink hot tea, and chat awhile about nothing in particular with the innkeeper. As twilight descended around us, quickened by the steep mountainsides that hemmed in the lodge on all sides, three Australian trekkers arrived at the lodge, placed their shoulder bags by the entryway, and joined us at the fire. After a few pleasantries and the obligatory comments about steep trails but lovely views, everyone grew silent and gazed into the flames. Occasionally someone rearranged the wood and coals in the fire to excite a brighter burn. Some time passed before the newcomers spoke again. "Well, they'll never find us here, mates," one remarked to the quiet room. They all then got up and went silently to their beds.

The sobriety of the simple comment, said in jest, I presumed, but with an edge to it, struck a chord in me. Indeed, no one ever would find them there, or me. Such complete anonymity and the severance of ties with everyday life are the seductions to which travelers succumb. Such opportunities provide a chance to discard, if only for a short while, life's attachments that seem to bind so many of us to an endless round of obligations, and allow an opportunity to enjoy the world on a grand and apparently limitless scale. Such promises fuel the tourism industry, even as it is determining the course of change in those places where it occurs. Our reverie in the darkened lodge was broken when, from the adjoining room, came the sound of cassette music and a new rock group from Down Under. The innkeeper recognized the music and knew the band's name; I did not.

The new breed of adventure travelers who crisscross the globe in growing numbers are hardly the commonly sketched tourists, loaded with luggage and opining national slogans, who search constantly for clean restrooms and a decent meal; nor are they the vagabond journeymen of bygone days, who forsook the sweet comforts of home for a bittersweet life on the road. Instead, today's adventure tourist is an intermediary product of an uncertain age and society, where wealth and leisure occur widely but without satisfaction; someone who seeks interludes where the conventions and common transactions of life are lifted. Many such tourists share a common, if unvoiced, sentiment that travel is intrinsically worthwhile and that the farther one gets from familiar places, the more interesting becomes the journey. In the process, such tourists become the spearheads of international tourism, the single largest industry in the world, and they are pushing the global economy to its outermost limits.

Those who seek the obscure routes and destinations, who actually relish the rigors encountered en route, will avoid the mass tours, where groups descend upon a destination like locusts, stripping the place as they devour it, remove it from the "must-see hit list," and review it all back home with instant photographs and home videos—the conquest of a new place where the trophies are memorabilia. But mass tourism still accounts for the bulk of international pleasure travel. Worldwide, tourism has increased tenfold since the 1950s. Nowadays, U.S. citizens traveling abroad spend several billion dollars a year. Such numbers are staggering, and to economists, enticing. However, the consequences of mass tourism for host people and places can be disastrous, particularly for those places that maintain strong cultural traditions or that host fragile natural environments. At the worst, ecological systems break down, social stratification occurs, materialism supplants older communal ways, market-based economies displace domestic subsistence ones, cultural decay takes hold. Places change. This is obvious to those who travel to well-worn destinations. It also is well documented in the scholarly literature on tourism and world development.

This book looks at tourism through the experiences and consequences of those who abandon the common tourist destinations and enter the more private worlds where old cultures remain intact, where the natural landscape is most pristine, and where the act of travel requires a high level of personal involvement. In describing the new type of adventure tourism, I consider its role in promoting change among host places. As a longtime participant in adventure tourism, I am obliged to look critically at my own experiences, to extend them beyond myself, and to see my travels as part of a much larger phenomenon that seems to be reshaping the distant places on earth. At some point my travels and my recollections of them joined with a growing awareness of the dilemmas of tourism development, a process outlined in various theories of tourism but articulated in the lives of those who do tourism.

Theories of Tourism's Threats

Many social scientists have only now begun to consider the pernicious role of tourism in promoting social and environmental change, and some have come to the disturbing conclusion that tourism is not the catalyst for development it was commonly thought to be. In a few brief lines, the poet C. Rajendra captures the critical perspective:

> When the tourist flew in
> the hunger and the squalor
> were preserved
> as a passing pageant
> for clicking cameras
> —a chic eye-sore!"[10]

The criticisms of tourism's role in many developing regions of the world parallel the much broader shifts in world political theory. How to incorporate such theory into the individual lives of the world's poor, who now host tourists in growing numbers and see tourism earnings as a means of obtaining economic prosperity, is a formidable task. Many scholars recognize that the purely growth-oriented forms of economic development sponsored by various "trickle down" modernization theories are seriously flawed. After decades of investment throughout the developing world, these policies simply do little to achieve their goal of a well-distributed increase in prosperity. The flow of wealth is a trickle indeed, and it vaporizes much too quickly, all too often into the pockets of politicians, the accounts of astute entrepreneurs, and the furnishings of a bureaucrat's flat. While the urban economies of Third World nations do capture some of the foreign earnings brought in by tourists, little escapes to the countryside. A result is the emergence of tourist loci, places where the bulk of economic transactions occur and where tourist services generate the greatest earnings.

Such a place is Chiang Mai, Thailand, a prosperous town in the northern part of the country adjacent to the remote hill regions and the infamous Golden Triangle. For travelers heading north from Bangkok to the rugged hill villages for trekking tours, Chiang Mai is a required stop. Tour arrangements for the tribal areas are completed here and the necessary contacts are made. Two decades ago this region, known for its diverse ethnic groups—Karen, Lao, Akha, and others—and for the cultivation of opium poppy, which supplies the illicit international drug trade, was frequented by few Western tourists. In the early 1970s, the region became popular among tourists on the long overland journeys through Southeast Asia. By the late 1970s the numbers of tourists had grown considerably and the tribal villages near Chiang Mai became common secondary destinations. In the villages, travelers were provided with simple lodging—usually in the village headman's house—food, and opium for those who desired it. Word spread among travelers, and by the 1980s the villages around Chiang Mai, such places as Meo Doi Pui and Mae Hong Son, were saturated with tourists.[11] Trekking to the tribal villages is now a mainstay in the local tourism economy. Most visitors to the region remain for a few days in Chiang Mai, where they find inexpensive guest houses, Western restaurants, shops, and nightlife. While a considerable amount of money is spent by tourists in Chiang Mai and to a lesser extent in the surrounding villages, the proportion of people who economically benefit from it remains quite small. A few people, however, are getting rich and most of them live in Chiang Mai.

Against the growth-oriented policies that characterize conventional international tourism and that predict the emergence of tourism loci, like Chiang Mai, that will capture the bulk of tourist dollars, alternative theories of development exist that aim toward more sustainable and distributive forms of economic growth.[12] These alternatives call for national development programs that control the negative effects of economic behavior on the environment and on local cultures. Conventional tourism encounters skepticism among some scholars and policymakers precisely because its impacts are not necessarily, or even probably, sustainable or benign and because, as one scholar wrote, "There is no other international trading activity which involves such a critical interplay among economic, political, environmental, and social elements as tourism."[13] But tourism is not solely an economic transaction, nor a thing detached from the experiences of the travelers themselves; indeed it is by just such experiences that tourism is known.

Most travelers I've met in remote places of the world share unexpressed, often conflicting rationales for their journeys. They are propelled into new frontiers of experiences that are at once intimate, personal, and ultimately self-absorptive. That makes it difficult to step back and imagine each traveler as a member of a much larger movement that has eventual global implications. Yet international tourism carries just such a prospect. Since tourists rarely study themselves and only occasionally one another, it is left to the scientists who study tourism to provide such a service—the abstraction, distillation, and analysis of innumerable personal quests of discovery. In the process, scholars have produced new tourism designs and patterns that both recognize tourism's negative impact and imagine a more positive role for tourism. These new models are often called "appropriate tourism" because they represent travel as a means to foster understanding and to establish meaningful cross-cultural encounters. They also seek to promote a more equitable distribution of tourism earnings for the local people who are involved in the tourism business. Alternative tourism may be a counterculture reaction against mass tourism, or it may be a reaction against the exploitation of the developing world. It assumes various guises—ecotourism, ethnic tourism, adventure travel, responsible tourism. And it is hotly debated as either an economic savior or a Trojan horse.[14] Only recently have I come to consider my own travels and those of fellow tourists from this wider perspective—viewing tourism as a social and environmental activity as well as one of leisure and adventure. In such a view, the question that looms significant is not necessarily where one travels but how.

Errant Journeys

The Pleasure Periphery

Global tourism has a long and colorful history, arising like a phoenix out of the obscure accounts of early world voyages of discovery. Dusty volumes with now ridiculous sounding titles, such as "Savage Races of the World," described indigenous people in either romanticizing or deprecating ways. The places that the natives inhabited were similarly portrayed with gusto as lands of adventure, stealth, and intrigue, offering enough mystery to satisfy the most demanding vicarious traveler. A few readers were so motivated as to launch voyages of their own to such places, inevitably booking passage on ships and, later, planes heading south. The books of adventure located in the back corridors of most town libraries still hold sway over romantic minds and propel people into the world's remote lands.

Nowadays, a large proportion of international travel is directed to the developing regions of the world, mainly to the tropics and subtropics. The reasons for this are many and complex, but include the equable climates and spectacular scenery found at many tropical destinations, as well as the rich cultural and natural heritages that appeal to visitors. But the appeal of such places is greater than the geographic qualities found there; it issues from what appears as the non-modern "other" in the face of the industrial, modernized home of the traveler. The tropics and other Third World regions command the attention of the tourist brochures, the travel magazines, and the posters of one of the richest sectors of the international economy—tourism services. The onslaught of literature that describes in fanciful ways the world's exotic places, and the success with which it does so, is astonishing. These promotions, together with the availability of cheap labor and land and other economic incentives for tourism developers, make tourism one of the most enticing industries in the Third World. But while the lure of tourism for host regions may be primarily financial, it is the discovery of places, imagined or real, and the exotic and personal awakenings that they evoke, that attract the travelers. The promise of discovery lies heavy in the minds of the tourists and ultimately on the landscapes of their journeys.

Nowhere in my experience can one find a richness of color, an assault on the senses, and an ease of being to match that of the tropical regions of the world. The fact that colonial histories and circumstances of nature, society, or present-day politics determine that these locations contain most of the world's poorest countries ensures that adventure tourists meet world development in an awkward embrace. Tourism scholars have named the tropical places where international tourism occurs the "pleasure periphery," implying for those locations some marginal position in the world economy.[15] It is useful to explore this idea further because it helps to identify tourism's impact on world development and to define for adventure tourists and their hosts the nature of their relationship. Such impacts and definitions may not be realized by tourists themselves, or immediately by their hosts, but they are inescapable facts of world tourism and their long-term association with prospects for development makes them doubly important.

It is widely believed that the nations of the developed world, where most international tourists originate, dominate the appropriation of world tourism earnings, reflecting the well-entrenched position of these countries in the global economy. The concentration of tourism-industry support, from cruise ships to rental cars, and the wealth that accrues to the industrial economies that service this industry, confirm this as fact. As a result, the physical flow of tourists and the financial flow of tourism earnings is decisively skewed to benefit the West, although tourism is promoted as an economic "leveler" for Third World regions.[16] Spatial models of tourist flows predict the direction and intensity of tourism activity. They show a pattern wherein tourists move from the generating areas located in the West, through intermediate gateways, and on to the final destination located in the non-West. For conventional tourists, the final destinations are often self-contained resort enclaves; for adventure tourists they are less-developed locations that offer unique opportunities for cultural or natural experiences. If we could see the world in all its humming movement, tourists would be only one species on the move, but a colorful and busy one, whose journeys are longer than most, drawing hazy, multihued arcs across the sphere of the earth. Such arcs connect the swinging gateways of world financial flows, and their tailings pile up at the doorways of the Western nations.

The tourism models developed by scholars are called *structural models*, or *core-periphery models*, borrowing some political economists' construction of a tripartite division of the global economy: a core located in Europe, North America, and other scattered Western countries, where industrial economic development is primary and successful and where wealth is accumulated; a semiperiphery occupied by economically emergent countries that cannot seem to exchange their traditions for foreign earnings fast enough; and the world periphery occupied by most of the world's poorest countries, where people live their lives according to older ways and softer rhythms, caught in the midst of poverty but maintaining cultural integrity in spite of the angst of knowing that to gain in one area undoubtedly requires a loss in another. This is less a spatial division of the world than a structural one, based on relationships that define access to power and wealth. But the periphery nations mainly occur in the tropical South. The relationship, or rather the linkage, between core and periphery, often serviced by the entrepreneurship and trade of the semiperiphery countries, is strengthened by international tourism, which solidifies the transference of invest-ment capital between the global economic sectors. Among the subsistence economies of the Third World, where tourism now prospers, the new economic arrangements can be startling. It is difficult to imagine, for example, that an innkeeper in the moun-tains of Nepal, tending to tourists now, as well as sheep, is subsidized by the international financial community. Yet, increas-ingly, such complex economic linkages define the touristic ventures of the Third World. They combine the efforts of venture capitalists in the Western economies and the development of the non-Western world in an economic union welded by the tastes of tourists.

Leaky Tourism Linkages

Proponents of international tourism argue that capital transfers across tourism space are beneficial to the host countries because they are an important means to acquire foreign earnings. Others, however, associate tourism development with inequities that arise from "leakages" in capital transfers (such leakages occur because host countries must import costly technology and goods to support tourism), from foreign ownership of tourism's national and international infrastructures, and from promotional and transportational biases among tourist delivery systems that favor the tourist-generating areas. The development of resort enclaves, which are heavily capital-dependent, in many Third World countries clearly shows such trends. The spatial structures of international tourism predicted by the core-periphery models determine the extent and intensity of tourism impacts and may subordinate the development goals of Third World economies to the further consolidation of the global economy under the design of the Western economies. The control by multinational corporations of international air service and hotels concentrates tourist flows in these models through a hierarchy of transfer points, connecting the Third World resorts with the tour arrangers in the West.

These highly abstract ideas can be seen in the development of conventional tourist sites throughout the world. The tropical Caribbean, with its Club Med resorts, cruise ship ports, and shopping and gambling meccas, is a prime example of where the model described above holds sway. The impact of tourism activities on the island economies is so great and the control by local people over their design is so minimal that many places now have relinquished their own destinies. Perhaps nowhere is this more true than in the Hawaiian archipelago.[17] Each year over six million tourists visit these Pacific islands. Most limit their stay to the congested commercial Waikiki strip on the heavily populated island of Oahu, plus perhaps a one- or two-day visit to one of the "outer islands." The term *waikikianization* is used to refer elsewhere to rampant overdevelopment of tourist facilities, characterizing Waikiki as a rather sordid archetype of what is wrong with tourism. Yet few tourists to Hawaii are disappointed by what they find (most of them report that their experiences exceeded their expectations) and the tourism development agencies of Hawaii greet with glee such trends. The land and the native peoples of Hawaii are the victims. The Hawaii example, however, is limiting in that Hawaii is no longer a part of the world's "periphery," having come into the heralded Pacific Age with the patriotic investment of the United States and the financial investment of Japan (over two-thirds of Waikiki and much of the rest of tourist Hawaii is now Japanese owned.)

Elsewhere in the Pacific, the linkages noted in the structural models are fully engaged. Such places as Fiji, Tonga, and the Cook Islands depend upon tourism that originates in Australia, New Zealand, the United States, and Europe. The geographer Steven Britton reported that the colonial legacy of these island nations, reinforced by contemporary foreign investments, contributes to social stratification in the islands, to economic inequities, and to continued financial dependence on outside assistance.[18] With its dollars, tourism often brings problems. Western Samoa, one of Polynesia's oldest cultures, is a newcomer to Pacific tourism. In the summer of 1991 Western Samoa's national tourist bureau reported that in the previous year about thirty-five thousand visitors arrived in the islands, a 20 percent increase from 1980. Apart from a few hotels in the capital of Apia and a smattering of local lodges and historical sites on the main islands of Upolu and Savaii, little is provided in Samoa in the way of tourism development. It has not yet developed into a highly rated island resort destination.

The Samoan islands are of volcanic origin; from the surrounding ocean they appear as weathered domes rising from a fringing reef. The main inhabited islands of Western Samoa are Savaii, Upolu, and Manono, all of which contain some elements of small-scale tourism. The primary attractions of Samoa for tourists are its tropical landscapes and intact culture. Coastlines, beaches, interior rain forests, well-kept villages, and agricultural plantations attract visitors. Many of the more popular beaches and some of the waterfalls, blowholes, and cultural sites are marginally developed for tourists. A small fee, collected by local residents, is now required to enter many of these places. But the overall levels of development and investment remain low. The government currently is seeking advice on how to enhance Samoa's image as a tourism destination and on how to develop the facilities necessary to attract and retain some of the Pacific region's growing tourist trade. On my first visit to Samoa in 1991, I relished the fact that few tourists were in the islands and I could travel to most places without meeting other Westerners. The Samoan tourism bureau did not share my delight. Instead, it is actively pursuing various alternative tourism strategies, including the sale of run-down government hotels to Japanese investors who hope to unload jumbo jets of tourists from Japan for a new, non-Hawaiian Pacific experience. But the country is ill equipped to handle travelers in large numbers. Natural and social carrying capacities may easily be exceeded. The limited available services and the lack of experience among most Samoans in dealing with tourists combine to make any tour off the islands' main roads an adventure in cultural diplomacy.

During the past several decades, many visitors to Samoa avoided land travel altogether by journeying through the archipelago on sailboats. The harbors of Samoa's main islands, like many of the other Pacific islets, have hosted a fleet of yachters. They were among Samoa's first adventure travelers. Where masts and rigging silhouetted the tropical sunsets, pleasure craft berthed in the calm and protected waters of Samoa's leeward coasts. Occasional forays

ashore aboard small dinghies brought the tourists to the coastal villages, where they experienced island life for a few hours, re-stocked supplies, and returned to their boats to chart new waters elsewhere. The connection between the sailing tourists and island natives was slim indeed, concocted of chance meetings, a meal or two, and Jimmy Buffet lyrics. The yachters continue to visit Samoa, a popular stopover on transoceanic voyages that sketch the routes of the early Polynesian mariners. Their overall impact, however, remains low. In the mid-1970s, small numbers of more invasive, land-hugging travelers arrived in the South Pacific, where they hoped to find the colorful but elusive paradise of Robert Louis Stevenson, Paul Gauguin, Margaret Mead, and Marlon Brando. Many found, instead, the bleaker Pacific of Jack London and Paul Theroux. In Samoa, it is true that the tourists discovered rain forests, waterfalls, and empty beaches. But they also discovered a culture more conservative than any at home. The thoughts of nude bathing and "living off the land" that accompanied their paradisia-cal vision were abruptly dispelled by the puritan Christian ethic of islanders and by the strictly enforced code of land tenure that prevailed throughout the Samoa islands. Land in Samoa indeed is commonly held. But to participate, one has to be tied to the comprehensive system of personal relations that are drawn through centuries according to family genealogies and chiefly titles. Tour-ists simply don't fit into this elaborate cultural structure and most, recognizing this, bypassed Samoa for other Pacific beaches. Fur-thermore, many Samoans themselves realized that they really didn't *like* the tourists.

Samoa's fledgling tourist industry, based in the capital of Apia, now seeks to diversify its tourism resource base by promoting the islands' splendid tropical environments. Several governmental or-ganizations, as well as private institutions and individuals, currently consider nature-based tourism to be a partial solution to the often conflicting aims of economic development and the need for environmental preservation. The ecotourism designs advocated in Samoa are based on the experiences of Costa Rica in Central America, which has developed a tourist industry centered in its cloud forests; of Rwanda, which used its gorillas to attract tourists; and of Ecuador, where the unique fauna of the Galápagos Islands are now advertised in the travel promotion literature more frequently than in the scientific literature.

Recent environmental reports prepared by researchers affiliated with the South Pacific Regional Commission and The Nature Conservancy identify and describe Samoa's most endangered environments—the rain forests at Afulilo Falls, the Sa'anapu mangrove estuary, coastal marshes, lava flows and blowholes on the island of Savaii, highland forests and montane lakes, and many others. Recognizing the difficulty of organizing environmental conservation in such places, the authors recommend that Samoan villagers engage in small-scale tourism operations centered on some of these ecosystems. The intention is to show how preservation and profit can be joined within a complex arena of customary indigenous land rights, government policies, and economic incentives.[19]

In 1991, I visited many of the designated natural sites, several of which already were hosting small-scale ecotourism improvements. These were village efforts supported in many instances by various international conservation associations. In 1992, a year and a hurricane later, I revisited the sites and found widespread destruction from the hurricane but significant improvements from the villagers, mainly in the way of trails and limited interpretive facilities for visitors. By the summer of 1993 these improvements were in various stages of disrepair. Many of the trails through designated rain forest and along the preserved crater ridgelines were overgrown and indistinguishable from the surrounding jungle, the flimsy resthouses were beginning to decay, and the main tourism work of the villagers seemed to be collecting entrance fees at the roadheads. It is too soon to tell the consequences of such incipient tourism efforts, but they mark the future of many of Samoa's fledgling protected areas.

Ecotourism and Adventure Travel: Too Good to Be True?

It is not surprising that a nation's development planners would seek to capture a share of international tourism's billions of dollars in annual revenues. What is surprising are the myriad ways in which it is done. Some countries simply acknowledge that the development of resorts and the influx of tourists are necessary and worth the degradation of the environment. Good economy doesn't always mean good ecology. Other countries, Bhutan for example, have put stringent controls on tourism arrivals and on those areas that tourists are allowed to visit in efforts to safeguard the country's natural and cultural heritages. A growing number of places have come to accept the idea that tourism and environmental protection are not only compatible but can even reinforce each other. They embrace the promise that ecotourism holds for national development: that tourists can sensitively visit a place, promote meaningful exchanges with local people, and contribute to local and national economies with the money that they spend. Examples of financial successes do exist. In Nepal, Costa Rica, and Kenya, ecotourism leads the way in tourism foreign exchange earnings. The direct benefits from park fees and travel arrangements combine with indirect benefits derived from general tourist spending at the destinations to contribute in those places to the local financial coffers. In the tiny Central American country of Costa Rica, for example, where ecotourism competes with coffee as the country's greatest foreign exchange earner, about half a million visitors arrive annually. They spent 336 million dollars in 1991. Costa Rica's nature reserves and parklands show dramatic increases in the numbers of tourists who visit them. At Carara Biological Reserve located near the Pacific Coast, visitation rates increased from 5,603 in 1989 to

19,500 in the first half of 1992; in 1991, the coastal forests of Manuel Antonio National Park hosted 152,543 tourists, up from 36,462 in 1982.[20] Despite the tourism earnings that accompanied such visitor increases, the park budgets in Costa Rica remain small, less than a dollar per visitor, and the natural parks consequently fail to adequately manage for so many tourists.

A 1991 World Resources Institute report on *Policies for Maximizing Nature Tourism's Ecological and Economic Benefits* indicates that the successful contribution of ecotourism to national development requires many complex strategies: regulated access to natural areas and attractions, levies generated through park fees, public versus private partnerships in tourist endeavors, ultimate usage of tourism revenues, and the need for comprehensive planning. Each of these strategies presents a management issue for ecotourism. Furthermore, because ecotourism dovetails with "ethnic" tourism, where ecology-seekers are culture-seekers as well, the issues extend from managing ecological systems to managing cultural systems. As with all forms of economic development, the management of ecotourism means more than its intention. This is particularly crucial for ecotourism because it places new values on long understood environmental features as they become visitor attractions. In Kenya, where environmental resources are now tourism resources, each lion is now worth $27,000 per year, each elephant herd $610,000 and each hectare of land $40 instead of the less than a dollar it derives from agriculture.[21] Such economic evaluations of environmental resources for solely touristic purposes contribute, however, to the same reductionist vision that has jeopardized natural environments throughout the world. Ethnic views of the wild do not automatically translate to financial appraisals.

In Nepal's southern tarai plains, Tharu tribespeople for centuries have harvested thatch from the jungles that surround their villages to use for roofing material. Economists value this resource at about $1 million per year. But the Tharus place no such value on the material, mainly because it is invaluable—there are no alternatives. So every grass-cutting season in southern Nepal, the authorities at Chitwan National Park allow villagers into the park for a few weeks to cut grass for their homes. This type of cooperation is used in Nepal to show how parks and people can coexist. Without such concessions, however, the villagers would simply poach the grass, just as they poach the animals, particularly the rhinos, that regularly invade their agricultural fields located along the park boundary. Furthermore, the argument that the park provides employment opportunities for local people as guides and concessionaires loses credence when the majority of park jobs are held not by the indigenous Tharu people, but by the more influential migrants from Kathmandu and other Nepalese hill towns. Nonetheless, parkland development in Nepal is justified from a complex of perspectives that includes its potential for tourism earnings.

A park does not make a nature preserve, nor does it guarantee revenue from economic transactions. The personnel who manage the parklands and those who provide services to visitors define such functions. In a recent report published by the World Wildlife Fund (WWF), Elizabeth Boo documents ecotourism activities in five case-study countries: Belize, Costa Rica, Dominica, Ecuador, and Mexico. In addition to the obvious fact that all, except Ecuador, fringe the Caribbean Basin, the five countries also share a national interest in ecotourism. Several criteria were used to assess the contribution of ecotourism to those nations' development, including visitation rates, tourism impacts at national and local levels, promotion efforts, and tourism infrastructure.[22] Apart from Mexico, which receives over 5 million visitors each year, mainly from North America, the ecotourism countries report varying but overall fairly small numbers of tourists—from Dominica's thirty thousand nature tourists to half a million in Costa Rica. Only a small proportion of tourists visiting Mexico are ecotourists (about 10 percent); in Ecuador and Costa Rica, however, the proportions are much higher—over 75 percent in Ecuador. Moreover, the nature tourists tend to concentrate in only a few places, thereby contributing to change in those places much greater than their overall small numbers would suggest. And despite the large potential for local impacts, the contribution of such tourists to national economies is fairly limited. The accounting may change as the promotional efforts of the adventure travel industry increase, but this is at the risk of increasing visitation rates beyond the carrying capacities of visitor destinations. Therein lies the ultimate irony of ecotourism: it is promoted by both environmentalists and industrialists as beneficial for sustainable development, but if it ever achieves the significant growth that would mark its success, it will violate such sustainability. Recognizing this fact introduces the question of how adventure tourism places are created and maintained.

The physical additions of roads, lodges, restaurants, and communication facilities, as well as less tangible services such as guide and interpretive facilities, constitute the tourism infrastructure of adventure travel destinations. In the remote regions of the world where the various forms of adventure tourism occur, such features often are nonexistent and require substantial new investments by the national government, by the tourism industry, or by local people. Within a single parkland, such efforts can vary a great deal in terms of capital outlay, design, and intention. Nonetheless, they constitute a primary feature of the tourism landscape. Perhaps more important than physical improvements at an adventure destination are the promotional images created to make that destination attractive to such tourists. The selection by tourists of adventure places is highly dependent upon how such locations are presented in the tourism literature. The words and the photographs that describe tours in the adventure travel brochures and catalogues interpret for the reader the desirability and authenticity of such places. Valued geographic attributes such as remoteness, lack of contact, aesthetic landscapes, and traditional cultures highlight the absence of amenities and contribute to a sense of authenticity. This is a very different type of promotion than that which is found in the mass tourism industry, which emphasizes comfort over authenticity and accessibility over isolation. Creating the images for adventure destinations is every bit as consequential as constructing the trails to reach them.

Inside Chitwan National Park in Nepal lies one of that country's most established nature tourism facilities—the Tiger Tops Jungle Lodge—designed to accommodate tours and individual visitors who come to Chitwan for wildlife viewing. The Tiger Tops compound is secluded by miles of jungle, and in this seclusion it offers tourists the rare blend of domestic comfort and wild animals. The cost of accommodations at Tiger Tops is high, reflecting the large capital outlay that was required to transform a jungle into a royal suite and the continued investment necessary to insure that the Tiger Tops experience continues to satisfy its affluent and demanding clients. This investment includes not only the well-appointed accommodations and gourmet food for which Tiger Tops is renowned, but also the expert guide and interpretive services that the nature tourists demand. Since the presumed interest of Tiger Tops tourists is to view wildlife, the resort maintains a fleet of elephants, jeeps, canoes, and walking guides to provide access to the jungle's hidden interior. Even when the animals are shy, Tiger Tops succeeds in satisfying tourists by bringing live animals to them. On some nights, bleating sheep are tied to trees near the lodge to lure that most prized and sought-after jungle resident, the Royal Bengal Tiger, into the tourists' range. The pitch black of a jungle night carries quite well the sound of a triumphant tiger, and even if the exchange is unseen by lodge residents, the night sounds of predator and prey satisfy the wilderness urge in most Tiger Tops tourists.

The five-star facilities at the Tiger Tops Jungle Resort Lodge, enjoyed by those who fly in from Kathmandu, cannot hope to serve the growing numbers of more casual visitors to Chitwan National Park (in 1975 only 2,206 tourists visited the park; by the early 1990s the number had increased to about 35,000). Most of the tourists stay instead at one of the simple huts that dot the landscape outside the park, concentrated around Saurha, a small agricultural village that now caters to international tourists rather than to the local farmers. The average spending of tourists in Nepal varies widely by accounting measures, but it is reported to be around thirty-five dollars a day. That barely buys a breakfast at Tiger Tops, but it covers several days in the Saurha lodges.

When I first visited Saurha, it was still a farmer's village, where the daily rhythms were punctuated by simple mealtimes, fieldwork, fetching water, and tending animals. In the mid-1970s, only a couple of thatch and mud huts existed where day visitors to the park could spend the nights. Food was available at the lodges, but it was basic—reflecting the grain and vegetable diet of the villagers. A few lodge-owners employed local guides (village boys with no formal training but with years of play and hunting experience in the jungle) who led tourists into the park by foot during the early morning hours and by elephant excursions to more distant park locations in the afternoons. One reached Saurha after a circuitous journey from Kathmandu—a rickety bus ride southwest, several hours along the hanging cliffs above the Trishuli River, on to the lowland town of Narayangarh; thence, a speedier bus ride to the small market village of Tadi Bazaar. From Tadi, it was necessary to walk or to ride a bullock cart the remaining few miles across open grain fields to the Rapti River and then on to Saurha, situated at the riverside. The journey always included missed connections, delayed or canceled bus departures, heat, and dust.

These days, the journey is basically the same as it was in earlier times; although Tiger Tops can be reached by air in a few minutes from Kathmandu, Saurha still relies on the buses and the bullocks. But the village of Saurha today is widely transformed. In 1990, over twenty-five lodges operated in the village. They have displaced homes and farm fields as they have expanded outward from the village center. The ubiquitous inns and the signs that advertise their business now overwhelm the village landscape. Almost everyone is involved in the tourist business. The dream of most young boys is to become a "first-class" park guide. The capital investments in agriculture have declined as they compete with tourism investments. Elephants almost trip over one another as they ferry the tourists to the park. During the dry season, the air is filled with the dust and noise of newly purchased tour jeeps that race through the village. Restaurants now serve beer kept cold in generator-driven refrigerators and belt out hit music from battery cassette players. Because Saurha exists now mainly as a staging place for tourists, not as a home for villagers, its function in the rural economy has shifted forever. From its agrarian beginnings, Saurha has become a service center for an international clientele. Many villagers can't remember when economic times were better, but others find that the good life, once centered on land and family, is gone forever.

Farming villages such as Saurha did not exist prior to the early 1950s. At that time, Nepal's lowland jungle was uninhabited except for the indigenous Tharu tribals who had retained a genetically adapted resistance to the widespread malaria that was endemic in Nepal's lowland plains. In the 1950s, however, a massive DDT spraying program eliminated the mosquito vector and thereby controlled malaria in the lowlands. This opened the way for a migration wave into the region from the Nepal hills and from the border regions of India. In the wake of the newcomers, trees were felled and forests were cleared to plant the crops. The immigrants, mainly members of the national Hindu caste system and politically powerful individuals, expropriated huge amounts of land for timber cutting and cash crop farming.[23] In the 1960s and 1970s, the Tharus became sharecroppers on their ancestral lands, working for a fifty-fifty split with the landed estates. Saurha now contains a mix of the tribal lowlanders and the more recent immigrants. For some Tharus, tourism has meant jobs. Others maintain their farming focus. But the wealth that has accrued to the tourism industry in Saurha has mainly gone to the already affluent Hindu elite. This dark fact begs the question of nature tourism's role for village development since a primary argument in its support is its perceived potential for fueling equitable economic growth.

In Nepal, Saurha now is widely known to be overcrowded with tourists, particularly during the pleasant weather and fine viewing months of winter, and for that reason it is avoided by many ecotourists. This avoidance mirrors that which is occurring among some highland Nepalese villages farther north, where the local economies have shifted almost entirely toward tourism. Adventure destinations such as Saurha and the heavily visited mountain trekking villages appear to undergo shifts in their desirability as travel destinations, and thereby proceed through a series of stages in the touristic industry. Butler has identified six of these: (1) a stage of exploration when a place is visited by few travelers and tourism facilities are virtually nonexistent; (2) a stage of involvement when the local people begin to accept tourists and provide limited lodging and meal services to them; (3) a development stage when tourism catches on, facilities become more developed, and the place is advertised in the travel promotional literature as a tourism destination; (4) a stage of consolidation and entrenchment when the local economy turns almost exclusively to tourism as its primary catalyst; (5) a stage when stagnation sets in, local environmental or social carrying capacities are exceeded, and artificial attractions appear; and (6) a stage of decline when the place loses its appeal in the tourism market.[24]

To categorize adventure destinations in such a way suggests that those places flourish for a period and then, like some kind of organism, die. This is misleading, of course. Adventure places do not function precisely in this way. They may degrade until they no longer serve the same kind of tourists, but then they may be instilled with a new vigor to serve new travelers. As a place develops a strong tourism infrastructure and begins to attract large numbers of tourists, its image is eroded for adventure travelers, for whom the absence of amenities is largely the appeal of a place, but its attraction for other, more conventional, tourists may increase. The sequence of tourism place development outlined above simply cannot proceed for adventure purposes beyond the stage when the numbers of facilities and visitors in a place remain low. If it does, the place will not remain an adventure tourism destination. This effectively truncates the linear development sequence for such tourism places. The peculiar tastes of adventure tourists, which highlight remoteness and the elusive ingredient of authenticity, demand that places maintain a low level of involvement in tourism development. This is fine for the tourists, but for local people and their national governments, it means that high levels of economic activity cannot be sustained unless the tourists pay *a lot* to visit them. The adventure tourism industry thus is caught in a balancing posture: promotion of tourism places is necessary to their success, but if overdone it will dispel the appeal of a place for tourists.

It is remarkable how quickly the adventure travel industry has forged persuasive images of adventure places and how extravagantly these today are presented to the tourist public. In 1975, I purchased in a London railway station a small typescript guide, the precursor to the Lonely Planet guidebook series, that informed me about the overland travel route between Europe and South Asia. It cost seventy-five cents and was fifty pages long. For thousands of young travelers like myself, embarked along this route, it was the only guide available. People bought it who were seeking adventures along untraveled roads. At that time, when Saurha was still a jungle village in Nepal, most visitors to the world's remote places traveled alone, assisted only by that simple first guide, by other written travel narratives, and by the tales of fellow travelers.

Adventure travel today, however, is a booming business. Almost every week I receive in my mail a new full-color, lavishly produced catalogue describing the new activities of an adventure travel outfit. The fact that such extravagant promotional literature is published at all tells the tale of economic success in the industry. Each year, Western adventure tourism entrepreneurs broker tours for hundreds of thousands of visitors to the relic places distributed around the world's periphery. Along the way, such tourism has become a vital player in Third World development, linking backward to ancestral places and wilderness cultures, and forward to future, undefined, lifeways. The modern beginnings of adventure travel can be best found not among today's adventure tourists, who mainly subscribe to the now established tours, but rather among the overland travelers of the past several decades who individually followed age-old routes that crisscrossed the continents and refashioned them into modern-day equivalents. Of these global routes, the Asia Overland Road, which linked Europe and South Asia for thousands of young travelers in the 1970s, was paramount—king of roads.

2
Along the Way

"I'm trying to get to Pakistan," I said.
"First you have to cross Afghanistan," the other said. He was little, bearded, and carried a guitar. "It's in the way, like."

— PAUL THEROUX, *THE GREAT RAILWAY BAZAAR*

A gathering of low ridges at the western foothills of the Hindu Kush mountains joins Afghanistan and Iran in a desert landscape known because of its stony brilliance as "the land of the sun." This empty corner of the Khorasan steppeland, a blank piece of the political puzzle of southwest Asia, appears on the maps only when the scale is rather large. The hills and the silence echo the region's past, the war cries of plundering Mongols, the chants of pilgrims en route to the temples at Mashed, the foreign tongues, and, more recently, the tinny music blaring from brightly colored buses, and the bomb explosions. To the northwest, the white volcanoes of Damavand and its sister peaks of the Elburz range stand sentinel over the naked landscape; the spirits that are believed by the local people to dwell on the summits gaze at a stream of traffic that has marked the route since at least the times of Xerxes and Darius. To the east are the sands and snow of the mighty Hindu Kush Mountains, whose name in Persian means *Killer of Hindus*. The mountains separate central and southern Asia, Zoroaster from the Hindu world, the Oxus River from the Indus, the "land of light" from the "land of infidels," familiar places from the unknown. The ruins of ancient

postal stations, caravansaries, and watchtowers, once connecting the distant empires of the Orient, are still discernible on the land. At the western end of the region is the Iranian town of Mashed, the city of martyrs, a place holy to the Persians for the fact that here three important men are buried; two were religious leaders of the Imam succession, and the third was a Tartar bandit and assassin. To the east of the passageway is the swaggering outpost of the legendary Afghan frontier. Within this broad swath of rocky earth and rubble-strewn villages is a seven-mile tract of no-man's-land, a slice of hostile desert unclaimed by either Afghans or Persians.

The domed mud huts and cantilever gates of the Afghan border, where the guards check travel documents with practiced skill and infinite patience, mark the eastern boundary of the neglected corridor. To the west is the Iranian border post, a stark and efficient concrete bunker set in the dunes. Scrawled in rough letters on the outer walls of the Iran customs house is a signboard with the following advice: "IF YOU ARE CARRYING DRUGS FROM AFGHANISTAN DROP THEM IN THE BASKET." Below the board is a shiny metal container. The interior of the building, where travelers are petitioned and searched, is gray and sparse. The masonry walls are pasted with a mosaic of tattered photographs showing tourists holding remnants of shoes and battered backpacks. Some of the articles are displayed next to the photos, torn apart to reveal where the chunks of hashish were discovered. The tourists in the photographs, manacled and under guard, were being carted off to prison. The message to would-be smugglers is clear.

A narrow ribbon of weathered concrete road winds among the low hills between the two border crossings. It connects Iran and Afghanistan for modern travelers much as the old Silk Route, of which this stretch of road is a forgotten relic, once linked ancient kingdoms for court emissaries and itinerant merchants. The Khorasan corridor historically provided a vital link in the Eurasian movement of goods and armies, but its significance today is diminished by the regional conflicts that plague the area. In the 1970s, however, prior to the rise of anti-Western fervor and Islamic politics in Iran and the tumultuous civil war in Afghanistan, a steady stream of Western travelers crossed this stretch of no-man's-land, traversing along the way a stretch of ambiguity in the region's political landscape. As in ancient times, the route is tricky because of the bandits, the meager supplies, and war; for the twentieth-century tourists, the rigors of medieval travel are repeated with each new crossing of the corridor. But the physical hardships of the crossing are transient, easily dismissed. Less fleeting are the existential shifts that occur among travelers when the short distance is crossed. The passage into Asia, which the Khorasan corridor physically and symbolically conducts, produces for travelers the classical confrontation between the safety of "home" and the uncertainty of "foreign." This confrontation is rooted in the psyche of Western societies and engages them, through scientific and humanistic dialogue, in the production of an image of the "Orient." Such a discourse locates the East in geographic, temporal, and cultural distances. Edward Said, in the introduction to his classic book *Orientalism*, states:

> We must take seriously Vico's great observation that men make their own history, that what they can know is what they have made, and extend it to geography; as both geographical and cultural entities—to say nothing of historical entities— such locales, regions, geographical sectors as "Orient" . . . are man-made. Therefore, as much as the West itself, the Orient is an idea that has a history and a tradition of thought, imagery, and vocabulary that have given it reality and presence in and for the West. The two geographical entities thus support and to an extent reflect each other.[1]

A Picture-Perfect Place

To say that in crossing the Khorasan corridor, modern Western adventure travelers pass through cultural as well as Cartesian space, figurative as well as physical landscapes, locates the route squarely in Said's conception of the imperial division of Occident and Orient[2]—a division that is based upon the European creation of the Orient as a sensual, cultural, and economic, as well as geographic, entity. For travelers, the journey from west to east, from West to East, is a rite of passage involving more than the linear distances. It causes a separation from known pasts and places, from earlier selves, and an ordination to a new world axis, confronting the "other," a faltering first step toward clarifying preconceptions about an unfamiliar part of the world.

In a real sense, then, the crossing is a test of the power and authenticity of maps already established in the minds of travelers. Such maps are more than lines and contours; they are filled with geographic imagery that identifies, within the spirit of adventure and the goal of exploration, places that are exotic and "picturesque." According to Linda Nochlin, the picturesque is pursued "like a form of peculiarly elusive wildlife, requiring increasingly skillful tracking as the delicate prey—an endangered species— disappears farther and farther into the hinterlands."[3] The value of "picturesque*ness*" is attributed not only to idealized and culturally valued perceptions of distant places but also to the perception that such places are on the edge of extinction, at a turning point where they no longer tie to the past but rather to the future. Nochlin continues: "The very notion of the picturesque is premised on the fact of destruction. Only on the brink of destruction, in the course of incipient modification and cultural dilution, are customs, cos- tumes, and religious rituals . . . finally *seen* as picturesque."[4] The prospect of "authentic" places skirting "modernization" (becom- ing less authentic), at the edge of destruction, losing their picturesqueness, propels both travelers and tourists to visit those imagined spots at top speed before the impending transformations are complete. Unfortunately, the tourists themselves often are the final blow, the ultimate consequence that hastens and finalizes the transition so disdained among those who now precipitate it.

The overland route to Asia, of which the Khorasan crossing is one segment, tumbles down from Afghanistan through the Khyber Pass to lowland South Asia, where a detour north takes travelers to the Karakoram Mountains and into a place called Kafiristan. Here, nestled among the spiraling peaks and gushing rivers of the highlands are three tiny tributary valleys—the Rumbur, Bumburet, and Bihir. The curious inhabitants of these isolated valleys, people who call themselves Kalash but are known to the surrounding Muslims as infidels, Kafirs—those "not of the book"—are thought to be descendants of Alexander's Greek army, a belief based on the fair complexions and red hair found among these people, as well as on the local lore that traces such a historical connection.

One thousand years separated the occupation of Kafiristan by fair-haired Macedonians and the later invasion of the territory by Tamerlane's Mongol army in A.D. 1398. During those intervening centuries, the land remained largely isolated from the rest of the world. But Tamerlane's invasion brought it squarely into global events. His army's march eastward across the Hindu Kush Mountains by camel and horse, and later by snow sledding down the precipitous ridgelines, finally brought it to the Kafir settlements, which they attacked, forcing the residents into Islamic conversion. Those who refused were executed and their skulls stacked into towers placed among the mountaintops.

The tiny Kalash valleys were spared the barbaric invasions from the surrounding mountains, and they remained among the last remnant places of non-Muslim Kafirs in Nuristan. The Kalash clung to their traditions with a gusto fortified by centuries of resistance. It was to end in the 1970s with a new invasion from the West—the overland travelers. Word spread first among the French travelers, then others, that here one could find a place unlike any other—"Man, dis place is *magnifique*, you know, very damn good." The Kalash valleys became a sort of Shangri-La and its inhabitants the lost children. No more.

From the intimidating frontier town of Dir, where the natives squatted along the dusty roads and picked their teeth with bush knives, up the dizzying switchbacks to the top of the snowbound Lowrie Pass, and into Chitrals' gun markets—weapon emporiums financed by drug smuggling and by the covert operations of the United States intelligence service—the overland travelers detoured to the Kalash country. There they discovered villages guarded by carved wooden icons, inhabited by unveiled women in Islamic purdah territory, laughing, and wearing colorful costumes and long strings of cowrie shells braided in their hair. They found also a people staring into the faces of their ruin. To paraphrase Kipling, "Come sir, join us on the road and I will sell you a charm that will make you the king of Kafiristan."[5]

The descriptions of the Kalash valleys spread from southern Asia to northern Europe along the Asia Overland Route, enticing travelers to get one last look before, poof! the valley cultures vanished. Which they did, partially in the wake of political agendas from Pakistan's capital of Islamabad, but mostly from the tourist trade. For purposes of promoting national unity and political control, Pakistan wished to more fully include its tribal minorities into the country's mainstream. This meant that the Kalash people had to forego much of their cultural autonomy—until Pakistan realized that the Kalash culture itself was a touristic resource. The Kalash valleys today resonate a "lost picturesque" and emanate a kind of poignancy all their own. Westerners arrive still in the valleys, not to discover things as they have been, but to find a relic place that once evoked powerful visions among Asia's overland travelers, imagery that eventually overpowered the place, leaving behind the consumed wisp of a former travel fantasy. I regret to this day my own visits to those valleys, enthralled by their beauty, naive, unaware that my own journeys would contribute in some measure to their demise. At that time, as a young man, I thought that the geographic images in my mind were exclusive, mine alone, and did not know that my travels would have a consequence beyond myself. As I later recounted my visits to the Kalash valleys to other travelers,

I inadvertently promoted them as tourism products and no doubt others visited there on my account.

The formation of such geographic imagery among travelers is tied to the oral and written travel accounts, to stories circulated among travelers that portray personal exploits as well as the geographic character of visited places. The anecdotes of modern travelers thus supplement the body of travel texts that have produced for Westerners an alluring concept of remote world places. In writing about Europe's eighteenth-century "planetary consciousness"—an awareness of distant places that was derived mainly through scientific explorations of the world, expeditions that were themselves framed by the colonial expansion of Europe—Mary Louis Pratt describes the 1735 international scientific expedition to South America led by the geographer Charles de la Condamine. The expedition brought back to Europe more than Cartesian measurements, specimens, or imperial riches:

> The tales and texts it occasioned circulated round and round Europe for decades, an oral circuit and written. Indeed, the body of texts that resulted from the La Condamine expedition suggest rather well the range and variety of writing produced by travel in the mid-eighteenth century, writing that in turn produced other parts of the world for the imagination of the Europeans.[6]

At the Edge of a Precipice

The Khorasan corridor linked for the overland travelers important segments of a visual and reflexive geography, a journey that ties together distinct experiences and places, continually defining and fashioning them into a certified travel route. While other segments of the Europe to Asia Overland Route also contributed to the travelers' sense of passage, of *accomplishment*, notably the Khyber Pass which transports one from the empty steppes of the Central Asia highlands to the teeming subtropics of South Asia, the peculiar circumstances of the Khorasan crossing, mainly its emptiness and harshness, mark it as a key transition in the journey to the East.

The fact that the route today attracts little attention obscures its coveted past when the corridor was under the control of successive despots and served as a primary artery between the East and the West. In 329 B.C., Alexander the Great and his army of Macedonians wintered on the empty plains along the Persian-Afghan border, awaiting warm weather to ascend the Hindu Kush Mountains to the east, en route to Taxila, now in Pakistan. The Greek army was camped there by mistake; Alexander's advance guard had misjudged the location of the Afghan mountains. Over a millennium later, during his extraordinary journeys from A.D. 1325 to 1354, the Arab geographer Ibn Batuta passed through the area collecting impressions of pious villagers and demanding chieftains, lamenting the fact that the local sheik, Qutb ad-Din an-Naysa buri, forced the sale of his Turk slave and hence imposed additional burdens on his arduous travels.

In A.D. 1382, the plains of Khorasan once again hosted military conquerors, this time the goatskin tents of the army of Tamerlane. For him, as for Alexander in earlier times and others who would follow, the corridor was a path to future conquests. Such conquests would later become, in addition to military, economic and even spiritual in their formation. Mercantile travel between the Mediterranean and Asia flourished along the route not long after the famous twenty-five-year journey of Marco Polo in the thirteenth century. Tracing the Silk Route sketched in the maps and accounts of the Italian merchant, the new caravans of traders, missionaries, dignitaries, and vagabonds crossed the region in search of the fabled distant lands. The guise of the Orient was thus impressed upon the European imagination, initiating a quest of discovery that began with the early world explorers and continues to this day.

The outlandish adventures of the mid-nineteenth-century Frenchman Joseph Pierre Ferrier, "Adjutant General on loan to the Persian

Army," marked the passage more clearly for the European literate. His popular account, *Caravan Journeys and Wanderings*, describes how he traversed much of Persia in disguise, not so much to escape notice as to avoid being mistaken for Russian or British, both of whom he despised with Gallic mistrust. Accompanying a small band of Persian pilgrims, robbed by bandits and harassed by customs officers, Ferrier made it through Persia to Mashed, where he quit the masquerade. To secure safe passage onward to Herat in Afghanistan, he obtained from Mohammad Wali Khan in the town of Mashed a letter to Sheik Jami, then governor of the surrounding district of Turbot, that read in part:

> May the most high, the most puissant, and most valorous Azi Rahim Khan enjoy perfect health. Then I have the honor to inform his high wisdom that at the present moment the most high, the General Ferrier Sahib, the companion of honor, the possessor of courage, and the cream of Christians, has been sent on a mission to Herat.[7]

In 1975, en route to Afghanistan from Iran, I crossed the empty frontier between the two countries, but without any similar letter. By then the stretch of road was legendary among the overland travelers who had left Europe bound for South Asia. It was a dividing line between worlds, the edge of a precipice, still a misconstrued place in most travelers' mental maps—imaginary routes constructed of oral and written narratives, not merely drawn by a cartographer's pen.

Rusty buses and third-class trains provided cheap passage eastward across Turkey and Iran to the border frontier at Islam Qala. From there, amid money changers, beggars, and ragtag hotels, a few ramshackle buses ferried migrant workers and itinerant merchants across to Afghanistan; but for the Westerners, outside the local system, no reliable public means existed to convey travelers across this last bit of unnerving terrain, a short stretch of road that

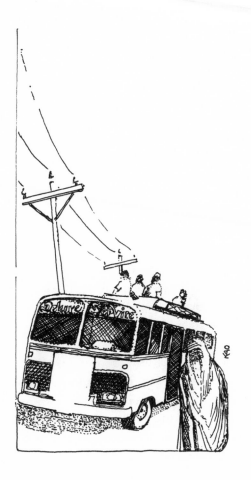

for many separated the East from the West, the known world from the mysterious places of Asia. To walk the distance, I was told, was to risk sunstroke, blisters, jackals, or even bandits. The Persian buses did not stop for the tarrying foreigners (the Persian word for *foreigner* also means *wretch*).

A group of young Western travelers were crowded around me, all dressed in the lavish tribal garb of the "Asia overlander." We had gathered at the Western crossroads like our gypsy predecessors, squinting across the desolate hills to the rising sun, and couldn't imagine the way across. But each day throughout the 1970s, a battered Mercedes bus, painted in psychedelic hues faded from the sun, jolted up the road and stirred dust and hopes among the tourists. The driver was a bearded, middle-aged German, a renegade from the postmodern world, who spoke rough English and charged the Afghan equivalent of a U.S. dollar for a one-way fare. His world was that desolate seven-mile stretch of broken concrete. He slept in the bus at night between countries and between worlds; rumor held that he owned no passport. The driver was porter for thousands, a crucial bridge in the steady flow of Westerners who sought among the ancient places of Asia the adventure, insight, sensualism, or escape from societies that increasingly failed to measure up to new evaluations. But without a proper visa, sufficient money, or the emotional courage to leave, he was caught there—hostage to the road.

The impulses that led to the Asia Overland Road were many, but the travelers shared in the pursuit of the elusive picturesque. Squinting across the barren stretch of the Afghan territory in the company of others not unlike myself, I felt a camaraderie that remained unstated and inexplicable. In his attempts to understand the motivations of tourists, the sociologist Erik Cohen described several types of them, among whom the budget Asia travelers occupy a lowly rank. They often are disdained by the countries they visit since they spend little money and linger a very long time. As cultural ambassadors, many prove to be an embarrassment to the countries of their citizenship, or at least to the image that the country wishes to promote. Nomads in a technological era, they seek a simplicity in their lives, which they measure by the size of their backpacks. Unlike conventional tourism, in which the goal is recreation, the overland traveler is interested mainly in the act of the journey itself. Cohen describes such tourists in this way:

> This type of tourist, corresponding to what has been called the adventurer or original drifter: rejects his home society and culture and seeks in the strangeness of the world of others, at the very least, experience of real, authentic life. At the most, he is in quest of an "elective centre" which will become a new spiritual home to him, an alternative to that modern world which he has rejected. He therefore travels by himself or in small groups, in an unhurried manner, spontaneously changing his plans according to his interests, disposition, and opportunities. As it was for the traveler of earlier times, travel is "work" and not mere "leisure."[8]

It is true that the overland traveler often tarried and the journey was not punctual, but the seeming spontaneity was guided by the fact that across the globe, in the most uncommon places, travelers were tracing in the unknown territory that lay ahead the routes of their (in)famous predecessors. The early world explorers thus set the imaginative pathways for contemporary adventure tourists. In their own quests for outward experience and inner meaning, modern travelers may extend the old routes and fashion them to new travel tastes. But to say that the nature of travel and the type of traveler to roam the Asian continent, indeed the routes themselves, have changed surprisingly little over the centuries is to discount the multifarious experiences and impressions contained in the act of travel. Each person's journey remains a uniquely singular feat.

Yet Ferrier's description of the nineteenth-century Persian gypsies as wanderers, colorful people who lived with nothing, detested a regular home, defied convention, wore colorful but dirty clothes, and followed their whims, portrays as well many of the overland travelers of the 1970s. Such is the perception others have of them and it is one they have of each other. It is the pattern of gypsies everywhere to carry their culture, to entertain where they travel, but also to cause mischief and even grief. Modern travelers see their designs in the world's early explorers, but bring as their inadvertent gift to the places they visit the contemporary society of the West. As with the early wanderers and the voyages of discovery, the drive for exploration and adventure among the modern adventure tourists derives largely from the needs of the time.

The pull of new travel frontiers, therefore, remains as much the push from home—expansionist or rebellious ideas, imaginative geographies, disenchantment, or boredom. And like their predecessors, modern travelers find in this romance. The maps that exist in the minds of prospective travelers, ones that sketch the white spaces of *terrae incognitae*, compete with the contoured maps of modern cartographers, so that the words of Marlow in *Heart of Darkness* still ring true:

> I would look for hours at South America, or Africa, or Australia, and lose myself in all the glories of exploration. At that time there were many blank spaces on the earth, and when I saw one that looked particularly inviting on a map (but they all look that) I would put my finger on it and say, When I grow up I will go there.[9]

The road to Asia is littered with the relics of adventurers who have sought in the vastness of that continent something unattainable at home. They are the keys to the modern maps of today's adventure travelers.

The Asia Overland Route, like other important adventure circuits—the "Gringo Trail" in Latin America, northern Africa's Salt Road, Pacific Island hopping—is proscribed in part by the

European explorations of the past centuries. One of the most accomplished of Asia's explorers was the Swedish geographer Sven Hedin, who crisscrossed the continent so often that it required thirty thousand published book pages to recount his journeys. In April of 1886 he first left Europe on a Russian steamer bound for Iran. On arrival he bought a horse and traveled three thousand reckless desert miles on his initial exploratory trip. Later expeditions led to detailed maps, a collection of sketches and photographs, the three-volume *Transhimalaya*, the nine-volume *Southern Tibet: Discoveries in Former Times Compared with My Own Researches, 1906–1908*, fluency in eight languages, accolades from around the world, and the place in history that he was forever seeking.[10]

Hedin's legendary journeys through the mountain fastness of the Himalaya inspired legions of mountaineers and trekkers, who today search for the physical and spiritual release that the mountains promise. The inspiration provided by the early explorers and travel writers lies not in the guidebook details they may provide, but in the visions of the journeys that their accounts conjure in the minds of those who read them. Peter Bishop writes that the travel writer "becomes the *bricoleur*, the odd-job person, who creates a body of knowledge from the materials at hand." But more important, he sees "travel accounts are involved in the production of imaginative knowledges. They are an important aspect of a culture's myth-making."[11] Along the adventure travel circuits, where old myths are resurrected and new ones continuously formed, lie the experiences of a place.

Geographic Routes to Imagined and Real Places

The corpus of travel narratives that profile the tourism places and that consequently fuel the imagination of travelers has the internal coherence of a collage. Oral reports, photographs, written essays and narratives, and memoirs fit loosely together to fashion a journey. Some of the pieces are well known, published as popular

nonfiction or as guidebooks and essays, where they become part of
the travel literature; others are more obscure and appear as singular
advice or comments in the signbooks of cheap Third World hotels,
scrawled on restaurant walls, embellished as personal anecdotes to
be shared among travelers on the long bus rides or while waiting
together at the immigration posts. They point the way to celebrated
places and recommended routes, paint portraits of people and of
extraordinary landscapes. Adventure travel circuits thus are forged,
produced and reproduced, emboldened, by the oral accounts of
those who pursue them. The routes ascend mythic and spiritual
heights as they become mysterious trajectories to the world's sacred
places. Such accounts blend geography, history, experience, and
imagination in a visual and anecdotal account of the "road ahead."
Such a road connects places that are themselves imaginary and links
them into a linear geography that becomes the landscape of the
journey itself.[12]

Where adventure travelers eventually go and how they manage
to navigate en route are questions that the travel industry itself seeks
to answer, or predict, through its literature and advertisement
campaigns, in its quest to turn a tourism profit. The alternative
travel guidebooks, which are fashioned after the eclectic and mostly
solitary tastes of adventurers and indeed often are written and
produced by them, emphasize the details of travel, but they rarely
promote places as commercial products. They do, however, write
the script for a new text of tourist landscapes, one that shows people
to an itinerant world that is argued in the alternative travel books
to be more authentic than the destinations covered by the conventional tourism guides. The impact of the latter on adventure
travelers ironically is contrary to their very goal—rather than
attracting adventure travelers, the commercial promotions repel
them, and in doing so inadvertently locate for them the undesirable
spots which must be avoided if "authenticity" is ever to be achieved.
The stable of travel guidebooks, its range of offerings from Fodor's
to Lonely Planet, shows the competing images of world places, and

it tracks tourists along parallel but often convergent paths of discovery. The power of the alternative guidebooks that are geared to the adventure travelers is apparent by their profusion in bookstores and by the fact that they are among travelers' most valued possessions. Central to the original design of a journey, the guides also are constantly consulted along the road. The books point tourists to the overlooks of unknown places, show them the view and sometimes the way in. The most popular series of adventure guidebooks, Lonely Planet, began with a single typescript itinerary describing the route from London to Delhi.

The Lonely Planet series, whose overwhelming success now mocks the name, contains 115 titles and covers most places on the globe, extending geographic coverage not only to the "lonely" spots but also to the crowded tourist places by contributing new thematic entries into them. Since the books are written by adventure travelers themselves, they impart to the reader an assured sense of authenticity. The books ask readers to provide updated information, to keep the books timely but also to create among readers a sense of participation. The guidebooks are bought in the West and carried to the non-Western world, where they are read, traded, sold, photocopied, dissected, and discarded—consumed, as the places themselves are consumed—"I can check that place off my list."

The contemporary adventure travel circuits thus are created and sustained in part by the proliferation and steady use of such guidebooks. In my own attempts to travel without them, a conscious measure to disassociate myself from the stream of travelers, I have at times felt abandoned, dislocated, somehow missing the boat. Then I would see the steady procession of tourists, crowded in buses and on train platforms, at rest in restaurants and public parks, threading along crowded alleys, hunkered over the same guidebooks, eyes peeled to the same dog-eared pages, the textual description of the place at hand winning their attentions from the direct experience of it, and my hesitation would vanish.

Adventure travelers also make use of other, older cairns and guideposts located along the routes of their journeys. These markers are illumined by the historical accounts of early explorers, records that provide narratives of those early exploration routes that now guide the modern travelers—as pseudo maps into the exotic world and as references against which contemporary experiences can be measured. Old and new stories shared among travelers, narratives of the journey, establish complex circuitries of adventure travel. These may appear initially as indistinct and incoherent references to selected places, towns circled on a map, roads to be avoided, recreational spots. But cumulatively they define a tourism space. In his study of the mythic creation of Tibet as a sacred travel destination, Peter Bishop wrote:

> Most travel accounts consist of small islands of personal narrative afloat on an ocean of dates and geography. These well-structured stories are often threaded together into a sequence which is entirely dependent on the idea of *route*. The image of the *route* emerges as the key to their apparent coherence and authenticity. Even the personal experiences of the traveller are secondary to the coherence and logic of the route; the route gives the traveller the authority to narrate.[13]

The imprint of imagined routes extends well beyond the minds of travelers to lie heavy on the landscape. When a route becomes popular, the flow of tourism traffic increases. At critical juncture points, known markers in the travelers' world, the concentration of tourist support in the local economy can be overwhelming and exclusive. Such places become stopovers, nodes in an emerging network of tourist movement. Opportunities for lodging and food at such spots are recommended and passed along the travel circuit by word of mouth and by guidebook. The legitimate creation of central places occurs at such nodes, focal points in an evolving tourist landscape and places of recovery for travelers grown weary of the long road.

Along the Way

The Way East by Overland

The Asia Overland Route, which during its peak in the late 1970s hosted thousands of Western travelers each year, but which now, circumvented by regional warfare, remains largely empty, illustrates how the construction of a travel circuit blends time and geography into a network that spans the continents. There is no precise origin for the journey, either as a point in space or as a moment in time, since it takes initial shape in the fascination with which Europe has viewed Asia since at least the period of colonial expansion. The traditional travel routes that connect the two continents, dating back millennia for regional trade and war purposes, became more firmly etched in the Western experience with the European explorations and mercantile trade that followed along them.

The more recent expressions of our romance with the Orient began midway into the twentieth century with the avant-garde travel writing of wealthy or leisured Westerners. By the time of my first visit to Asia in the mid-1970s, a spiritual and sensual fascination with it had developed among Western travelers. Its appeal was based partly in the imaginative works of such novelists as Herman Hesse, Graham Greene, and Somerset Maugham, and in the memoirs of Asia's intrepid explorers. Its imagery is contained in the photographs of picture books and magazines, the analyses of anthropologists, and the tableaux of the painter Delacroix and the photographs of the Michauds. Its resonance derived from the scriptural interpretations of Hindu, Buddhist, and Islamic scholars that preoccupied the minds and spirits and infused the geographical imaginations of Westerners. In other words, the Asia Overland Road was paved in the history of a multitude of individuals wrestling with the meaning of the "Orient" and their relationship to it.[14]

Many of Asia's seekers, propelled by both the earlier visions and more contemporary definitions of the Eastern mystique, were in search of Shangri-La, Shambala, an ambiguous and mystical place that occupied the traveler's mind. Thomas More coined the term *utopia*, a reference to the fleeting place unattainable except perhaps in the imagination. The term and the idea it conveys provide powerful inspiration for adventure travel. Because utopia is so elusive, so unattainable, so inviting, so mysterious, it is sought after in the world's most remote and difficult places, the "ends" of the earth, rather than close to home. It is not necessary to fully understand what utopia means, other than to know, "as every schoolchild knows, utopia is both no place and a good place."[15]

The modern Asia Overland Route, utopian in its initial conception and ultimately its circuity, a guided but random journey to mystical places, took shape among adventure travelers within a few short years, amidst people intent on breaking the ties that bound them to a disaffected past and on grasping their own private *fata morgana*. The literal consolidation of the overland route was enhanced in the 1970s by the efforts of European brokers who established transport companies to ferry travelers from Europe to Asia aboard the famous "Magic Buses." Those loudly painted, boisterous rides across the southern rim of the World Island acclaimed the attention of "a movement," a hip happening of Eastbound seekers of Asia's mysteries, celebrated by rock musicians and chronicled in the pages of the alternative press. The buses attracted travelers the way a beach collects driftwood, spontaneous yet driven by a powerful tide, and united them on a fantasy ride to the ends of the earth. They were the loud fringe of a much quieter movement, however, one in which thousands of tourists slipped silently through time and space aboard the local public buses, third-class trains, camel caravans, and walking trails of Asia.

The overland road to India and on to Kathmandu, Asia's premier attractions—the former for its tumultuousness and the latter for its peace—began in the railway and bus stations, public parks, cafés, and hostels of Europe's northern cities. There, the youth of Western society converged and conferred on one another the collegial bond of travel. Alumni of Asia, travelers recently

returned after months on the overland road and exhausted from it, anointed those just departing along the eastward track with advice about exchange rates and black market deals, with talismans and puffs of hashish smuggled across innumerable borders, and with scribbled maps leading to lost cities, monasteries, and the Valley of the Flowers.

The circuitous way to Asia led first through Europe, from the initial points of departure in London, Paris, or Amsterdam, southward across the northern European lowland to the Alps, on to Yugoslavia or through Italy to Brindisi, and from there by ferry through the Ionian islands to Patrai, Greece, in either case leading to souvlakis and ouzo in the quiet parks of Athens. That city was a major point of departure for travelers heading to Turkey and Asia Minor. The trains that ran northeast to Thessaloniki and across the Grecian panhandle joined with the boats across the Aegean Sea to ferry a steady stream of adventure travelers into the gateway city of Istanbul, Constantinople, Byzantium, the acclaimed heart of the Ottoman empire. The Europe crossings, accomplished by commercial carriers aboard the "Magic Buses" or by hitchhiking, was the first step on the long Asia Overland Road, but many travelers intent on reaching the East were left behind in the West.

The pull of home, the pleasures of Europe, the trepidations of unknown Asia, all accounted for the high attrition rate. The crossing from Greece to Turkey on the Thracian land bridge, the narrow peninsula that separated Europe from Asia, West from East, thus held special significance for travelers for whom it symbolized a first break with the familiar world. This would be repeated along the route many times, among the Khorasan steppes, which for many symbolically divide East and West, and later at the Khyber Pass, which empties from the brown desert wastes of central Asia to the crowded greenery of the Indian subcontinent. A psychologist, interpreting the subconscious impulses of travelers, wrote:

To cross the border, in the unconscious, means to separate: hence the anxiety accompanying border crossings (separation anxiety). On the other hand, it means uniting with the new, good mother: hence the elation, and later the disappointment.[16]

The idea of discarding a known world to embrace a new one, with all the anticipation and gathering restlessness that it engendered, proved unsettling enough for so many that by the time Istanbul appeared on the travelers' maps, the tourist ranks were dramatically thinned. Those who continued en route, with almost dogged determination, quickly discovered that they were not alone in their sometimes boisterous, often solemn, march to the East.

The mosques of Istanbul, dominated by the splendid Hagia Sofia and Blue Mosque, punctuated the city's skyline, draped a Moorish silhouette over the tenements and streets, and shadowed the small cafés and cheap hotels where travelers met to drink the thick sweet Turkish coffee and to lay plans for the continued journey eastward through Turkey. The city provided an early glimpse into the fabled Orient: dancing bears wearing manacles, a grimy waterfront, the jewels of Topkapi, pickpockets, the waft of unfamiliar spices and incense, a vaulted marketplace, a den of dark alleyways, wizened faces, silk, and silver merchants. In its landscapes and architecture, Istanbul showed a history of conquering empires that connected centuries and three continents—the Christians and the building of the Roman world, the Byzantine Empire, the Turkish Conquest, Ottoman, and modern Turkey. The travelers to Istanbul confronted these layers of its history in the monuments, churches, fortress walls, aqueducts, and columns of the urban landscape, in the diversity of languages and food, and in the faces of town dwellers. The city was a gateway to antiquity, to old lands and civilizations that only grew more ancient to the east. Travel in that direction crossed not only distance but also time.

Istanbul thus had one foot in the Occident and the other in the Orient, one in the present and one in the past. By day, the city was foreign but inviting, by night, mysterious and dangerous. This duality of Istanbul's character was heightened by the two-way flow of overland travel, where the eager and apprehensive eastbounders met the returning seasoned veterans of Asia. The distance between the two groups was discernible. Those heading home, to the West, wearing Pakistani robes and silken scarves from India, adorned with strings of coral, turquoise, and Afghan lapis, met those going East, grew impatient with their naive questions, and grudgingly shared their hard-won knowledge with the new initiates.

At that time, one of my goals along the route was to reach its terminus in Nepal and hike through the Himalaya Mountains to Mount Everest. The little that I knew, or pretended to know, about that place I had distilled from the mountaineering exploits of those who already had assaulted the icy summit. My immediate plans were much more modest, to reach the base camp and to merely gaze upon the mountain. The look would encompass not simply Everest's black triangle of rock, but all of my fantasies about that mysterious sight, and indeed focus the awe-struck imagination of the entire Western world on the *axis mundi*, the symbolic link between heaven and earth that was physically contained in the soaring heights of that highest of earth's places. In Istanbul, en route east, I met a young man who had actually been there, had hiked from Kathmandu to Namche Bazaar, and then on to Kala Patar and the Everest Base Camp—a two-month trek that he graciously described to me in vivid detail, eyes flashing in his monk-like shaven head, a sparkle of excitement at his remembered experiences. The young man's only advice to me was practical and simple: "Take along several cans of fish for the protein you will need."

Although I was not to reach Everest on that first journey, I fumbled along toward it for many months, dragged onward by its image, enhanced by the lore of innumerable travelers, whose names I have long forgotten, and by a developing stratagem that now included stocking up on tinned sardines and tuna. Each chance meeting with a veteran of the Asia road opened further the possibilities for exploring *terrae incognitae* and indeed increased the very frontiers of my imaginary journeys. The experiences and the perceptions of others combined with my own, to enhance overall my illusion of the lands that lay ahead. The process of defining and redefining both the image of an unknown place and the strategy for exploring it is integral to travel and determines for the traveler the goal of geographical discovery. Moreover, as John Allen wrote, "What exploration makes known may expand in the imagination to encompass what remains unknown. Blank spaces are intolerable to the geographical imagination, and people are tempted to fill them with imaginative extrapolations."[17] Fantasy thus predates the journey and continually propels it along new courses.

Fashioned from distinct experiences, travel at first ravels discrete incidents into a tangled weave that becomes more refined only as the journey proceeds. The elements that most commonly linked the Asia overland travelers into a shared consciousness were the imagination of new lands and the effort required to reach them. With travel, fantasy based upon experience displaced that based solely on the imagination. This is the distance that separated in Istanbul the eastward and the westward travelers. It was known by both groups, mixing and intermingling, providing a strategy to the former and a certain contentment among the latter, a realization reflected in the words that I read scribbled on latrine walls in one of that city's dingy hotels, T. S. Eliot's observation that ". . . the end to all your travels and explorations will be to arrive at where you started, and know the place for the first time . . . " Eliot was right, of course, no one can return home unchanged. The only way left is forward. And I never knew who had copied those words: someone returning or someone going?

The options to leave Istanbul were three: it was still possible to catch one of the Magic Buses passing through from Amsterdam or Athens, pile in among the hippies, their cushions, and guitars and become one of the tribe; or one could take local transportation: journey by boat through the southern Black Sea along the Turkish coast to the town of Trabzon or by train to Erzurum through the rough eastern interior of the country. The former provided passage aboard leaky steamers for a pittance that included a night's sleep on deck (an important savings for those travelers who measured the quality of their journey by duration alone). The latter journey began across the Bosphorus from Istanbul in the western terminus of the Turkish railway system at Haydarpasa. If tickets were available, not a certain thing in the station where everything from the benches to the Ataturk portraits to the ticket master was severe and foreboding, second-class passage provided a narrow wooden bunk to climb onto at night and the opportunity to mix with local people over whiskey, strong cigarettes, and trick card games.

Travel east from Istanbul on the overland route thus diverged for a stretch in central Turkey, with some travelers heading north, others south to Anatolia, and a third group maintaining dead center, but all to reconnect again in Erzurum, an eastern Turkish town known among overland travelers mainly for its bandits. All transportation connections required a night layover in Erzurum, an inconvenience that made Erzurum a fledgling node on the overland travel circuit, which supported a few decrepit hotels sporting barred windows and written admonishments to stay indoors at night. Murder was commonplace and theft more so. The route consolidated in Erzurum to become a single thread stretched across the Kurdish countryside into northwest Iran. There were no violent civil wars in the landscape or camps of Kurdish refugees in the mid-1970s, but the threat of robbers was constant. So most travelers made a mad dash to Tehran, where they got hung up in the city's traffic.

When the Shah of Iran occupied the Peacock Throne, a grand seat stolen from lands farther to the east, he governed a country that had a rich history but a poor peasantry, a country with the military hardware of the Space Age, thanks to the United States, but the rural economy of a despotic age. Iran's cities, where the country's growing middle class lived, showcased the country's oil-based wealth. Such cities grew rapidly in the 1970s, with no planning. Tehran in particular showed the strain of too many cars and people, but few roads and parks. Its new buildings, designed for office efficiency or for show, were sterile places that overwhelmed the city's more traditional architecture. Tehran held little of interest for most overland travelers, was despised actually for its modernity, and so it served mainly as a transportation gateway where buses could be arranged for the onward journey to Mashed in eastern Iran.

From there, the crossing into Afghanistan via the empty Khorasan corridor transported travelers through a metaphorical, as well as political, frontier, through ethereal and terrestrial space. It took them to Herat, where a scattering of small hotels served those en route north to Mazari Sharif or south to Kandahar and then on to Kabul. A third passage from Herat, one that traversed the central highlands of Afghanistan, could be managed on horseback by joining a trading caravan. I never saw again the few travelers I met in Herat who embarked on that interior route. Apparently, their journeys, if successful, were much delayed. In my own northern crossing of Afghanistan, en route to the ancient trade post of Balkh on the steppes of Turkestan, I traversed an uneasy landscape of feudal wars, unfettered nomads, farming villages, and miles of open space. The desert landscapes that prevail in Afghanistan contain the extensions of the Dasht-E-Kavir desert to the west and the arid uplands of Baluchistan to the east.

Traveling northeast from Herat, crossing the fertile valleys of the Hari Ru and Murgah rivers, the rutted dirt track passed along the northern foothills of the Hindu Kush Mountains and skirted the borders of Turkmenistan and Uzbekistan, new independent republics of the former Soviet Union that share old tribal ties with the Afghans. Except for the river valleys, which are lush irrigated oases, it is a vast, generally inhospitable terrain, the country's northern heartland, a landscape that bakes in the summer sun and freezes under winter's snow. Its visual component is sparse and redundant, Zen-like in its repetition of patterns and muted pastel colors.

Crossing it by bus one night, caught at the side after our vehicle careened into a dark hillside on a blind curve, the driver set tumbleweed bushes to flame to light the damage. In the turbans and the shadowed faces of the passengers milling around, I saw a scene that, minus the bus, was ageless, and my mind drifted over the lean hills to imagine where these people lived. The landscape seemed to my senses much deprived without the markers I knew, lacking something that would connect me to this place. Where were the symbols that make a landscape and give it meaning? Where were the sounds and the smells? Looking into that empty landscape, made light in the night's dark by burning tumbleweed and a waxing moon, I felt myself gazing into the impenetrable frontier of travel itself. I was a passerby; the landscape remained a backdrop, a place that I would never fully know.

That realization, prompted by the stereoscopic vision provided on a night bus through Afghanistan, affirmed in my mind the division between visitor and native. My view, bounded by the horizon, took in only the *horizontal*. That of my fellow passengers, all of them native to this place, unbounded, took in a stratified cosmos, the *vertical*, where the stars in the night sky above the wrecked bus were holes into heaven itself.[18] The Afghan passengers were at ease, at home. But for me, the absence of known markers in the visual landscape and of the other senses—smells and sounds that I could respond to—alienated me from this place. I kept looking at, smelling, listening to, the land in the hope of connecting with it and establishing in my own mind its validity as a place for me to be. Such a confirmation escaped me. I was never able to integrate fully the Afghan landscape into my own evolving sense of the world. That country remains for me one of the most elusive places on earth.

The road north to Mazari-Sharif, the central bazaar of the windswept Turkestan plains of ancient Bactria, led first to the town of Balkh, now only a ghost of itself—full of dirt and hidden mounds and crumbling fortress walls.[19] In its heyday, however, Balkh was the "mother of towns," a thriving commercial market located astride the Eurasian Silk Route. The noted archaeologist Louis Dupree, a scholar of Afghanistan's prehistory, described the splendid trade along the Balkh route:

Major items of export from the Roman Empire . . . were gold and silver plates, woolen and linen textiles, topaz, coral, amber . . . frankincense, glassware, and wine. From India came cotton cloth, indigo, spices, semiprecious stones, pearls, ivory, Kashmir wool, steel swords, and furs. Central Asia contributed rubies, lapis lazuli, silver, turquoise, various gums, and drugs. China sent raw silk to Rome, and embroidered silks to Central Asia and India. Furs and gold from Siberia and Manchuria and many spices from the east traveled to both India and Rome.[20]

Westerners traversing Turkestan in the 1970s caught only fleeting glimpses—desert caravans, spices, rug markets—of the rich trade that marked the history of the region. The dust, the parched air and undying heat, or the bitter cold that prevailed for much of the year limited the explorations of overland adventure travelers and propelled them southward again to Kabul, the capital and largest city of Afghanistan.

During the time of the British Raj, when India was a colony of the English and Russia was controlled by the Tsars, Kabul was the seat of intrigue. Spies and secret emissaries of Britain and Russia furtively sought one another out among the nearby low hills and in the crowded bazaars of the city. In 1975, Kabul was still a place of intrigue, where the "Great Game" was played, not by the old colonialists, but by the new tourists. The popular thoroughfare for travelers in town was called "Chicken Street," and here congregated a notorious and volatile mix of Western and Afghan drug and gem smugglers, Pakistani gunrunners, convicts, spies, and international pleasure seekers. The ubiquitous cheap lodges and quasi-Western restaurants, the flimsy cinemas that showed Hindi dance films, the hashish dens, and the tunes of Radio Kabul served in varying ways the travelers who passed through the city.

The amenities and diversions of Kabul attracted travelers who quickly traded their dusty Western clothing for desert costumes at the second-hand clothes dealers that were so prolific in the city— a thriving business that had its origins in the 1930s when Amanullah, Afghanistan's modernizing king, forced Kabulis to wear Western clothing inside the city gates. Forty years later, more Afghans wore Western-style dress in Kabul than visiting Westerners. The change of cloth, however, was more than a matter of taste among the Western travelers; it was a rite of passage. In discarding their Western clothes, travelers symbolically shrugged off their societies. In adopting native dress, travelers did not become natives; that would be impossible. Rather, they demonstrated to other Western-ers that the passage from their own world to that of the "other" had indeed been achieved, a passage that deserved recognition and certainly a new look.

While from a distance the overland travelers appeared very much alike in their outlandish costumes, and indeed the motives behind the masks were similar, the distinctive fact about the wardrobes of the Asian travelers was that each was unique. The cut of the clothing expressed not only the character of the person but also the nature of the travelers' inquiries into the new material world around them—in Kabul's clothing shops were shepherds' embroidered leather robes, bazaar merchants' silk, traders' semiprecious stones, the mirrored and tie-dyed cloth of the desert—something, it seemed, for everyone. Western travelers donning Eastern garb were not dissimilar from the Afghans wearing leisure suits—both were

attempting to fit into a world that was not of their making. In most world places that would have appeared conspicuous; in Kabul it was only normal.

Travelers' needs to fit into the landscape, and to employ all their available senses to do so, appear to be in the nature of human beings. From our earliest childhood, we strive to make sense of our world, make it familiar to us, to know the land and its moods and our place in it. Many travelers feel a sense of accomplishment when they have achieved this in a brand new place. It is largely a personal achievement, invested in the values and views that we bring to a spot on earth. The geographer Yi Fu Tuan introduced the word *topophilia* to convey "the affective bond between people and place or setting." Such a bond is created by experience and by response to the environment. For Tuan,

> The response to environment may be primarily aesthetic: it may then vary from the fleeting pleasure one gets from a view to the equally fleeting but far more intense sense of beauty that is suddenly *revealed*. The response may be tactile, a delight in the feel of the air, water, earth. More permanent and less easy to express are feelings that one has toward a place because it is home, the locus of memories, and the means of gaining a livelihood [italics added].[21]

When I was a traveler on the Asia Overland Road, Kabul was never my home, but it has not left my memory either, and I suspect that it never will. Like myself, other Asia travelers felt a disconcerting connection to the empty lands of Afghanistan. It was not one of familiarity, but one of achievement and of the slow progression from fantasy to reality, from imagined places to experienced ones; it was the bond that is the very reward of travel—a covenant not only to a place but to a journey, and therefore it was far from fleeting.

Kabul was a place on every overland traveler's route. It was not to be missed—unavoidable. But few chose to linger there. The

68

strands of the overland route, which disentangled in Herat as travelers moved north and south through the Afghan countryside, wrapped again in Kabul before the drop to Jalalabad and across the storied Khyber Pass. From the west, the initial view of the pass was far from colossal; it looked like just another brown cleft in the bleak and repetitious hillsides. After only a few miles, however, the world seemed to give way, pulled like a rug from underneath, and the dizzying switchbacks that spiraled downward to the humid plains of Pakistan swept travelers literally off their feet.

Traveling the route in the 1970s, I saw in the hills little of the threat that confronted the nineteenth-century frontier forces of the British Raj, when the Khyber Rifles controlled the slot and treacherous battles were fought between the British and the local warlords.[22] A few years later, in 1980, I stood once again at the eastern end of the pass and looked west toward a country that was in turmoil, a place that I was forbidden to enter, where history repeated itself, and I remembered the journey of a few years before that I knew I never would repeat.

The descent of the Khyber Pass carried the overland travelers into yet a new landscape and a new world of the senses. It opened onto a spicy land, full of humidity, haggard beggars, and cow dung, reverence and bustling markets. Dumped into Pakistan at the foot of the Khyber Pass, the overland travelers tended not to tarry but to flee instead to the northern mountains for relief from the heat or across the plains of Sind and Punjab to India.

More than Afghanistan, which held its own interest, Pakistan for most travelers was simply in the way. Few lingered long enough among the landscapes of Pakistan to see in them the world's antiquity. The ruins at Taxila, marking the Indus Valley civilization, and the equally fine archaeological sites of northern Swat, showing the glowing age of the Gandara Buddhists, were but historical footnotes in a few travelers' diaries. Most were intent upon reaching India, a more recent construction than the Indus Valley civilization, and located further east. They followed the words of Mark Twain, who described India as "that land that all men desire to see, having seen once, by even a glimpse, would not give that glimpse for the shows of all the rest of the globe combined."[23]

Hearkening also to the mythical urgings of the Hindu deity Indra to wander and to the words of the Upanishads that promote in India a society of travel, the overland travelers were drawn to the country like moths to a light, compulsive but apprehensive. Every traveler knew that there was little ambiguity left in the minds of those who reached India—they loved or they hated it. The overwhelming urge for overland travelers was to see for themselves which it would be. The overwhelming fear was that they would not like it.

In her analytical study of Asian tourism, Linda Richter wrote:

> Interestingly, the exotic character of the subcontinent, which serves to attract many, may also repel others because of fear of the unknown and the unfamiliar. Moreover, India and other South Asian countries also suffer from what might be called the "begging-bowl" stereotype, an exaggerated image of mass poverty, squalor, and disease that continues to be perpetuated in political cartoons and other mass media in the West, particularly in the United States.[24]

Richter partly attributes India's allure for Western tourists to such promotional devices as the Festival of India exhibits that toured the Western countries and to such films as *A Passage to India*, *The Jewel in the Crown*, and *The Far Pavilions*. She noted that upon arrival, many tourists are pleasantly surprised to find luxury accommodations and nowhere near the squalor reported in the popular media.[25]

While that may be true for conventional tourists, the adventure travelers, by the design of their journeys and the places they frequented, found more of the reported squalor and were drawn more by the promises of such fanciful films as *The Man Who Would Be King*. India for travelers was to overcome discomfort, endless hassles, and the risk of disease, to conquer the inhibitions of the initiate, to attain the status of "veteran of the overland road," and to become a road warrior. Only then could the wonder of India be attained. Otherwise, its marvels and mundane mysteries remained hidden behind the cloak of exasperation that confronted all new travelers to India and confounded many of them so that they speedily left in various states of disarray, vowing to return again in the future when the odds would be on their side. For those who remained, the tests of India were accepted.

Hindu morality, the seemingly incongruous blend of logic and taboo, was a test for the travelers; the teachings of the Bhagavid Gita, summed in a phrase, tell us that "your business is with the deed, and not with the result." Indeed, for the overland travelers, the journey and not the destination was paramount. On a metaphorical level, the rigors of travel in India were in due course, part of "the way," and therefore in keeping with what India represented for the travelers. The basis of pre-Hindu Vedic religion was sacrifice; it ensured the transmigration of souls, the *dharma* journey, and provided a means toward salvation.[26] Intent upon some form of enlightenment, however frugal, the overland travelers withstood the onslaught of disease and deprivation in their (sacrificial) quest for spiritual knowledge. By birth beyond the karmic bounds of true Hinduism, Western travelers nonetheless saw in India and in their travels to Asia an opportunity to journey through the metaphysical landscapes of the Hindu world and in so doing overcome their own limiting worlds.

The disarming nature of India lies in its seeming juxtaposition of opposites—light and dark, violence and passivity, drab and intense color, bustle and lethargy. These are not unfamiliar themes. But India's integration of opposites is more than sensual; it is at the spiritual core of the place—an equilibrium that is invested in the notions of dharma and karma. In exploring this idea, the author

V. S. Naipaul wrote: "To arrive at an intellectual comprehension of this equilibrium—as some scholars do, working in the main from Hindu texts—is one thing. To enter into it, when faced with the Indian reality, is another."[27]

A compelling goal of overland travelers, people to whom Naipaul gives the notorious "hippie" appellation, is to come to terms with such a reality—in multifarious ways, sometimes successfully, other times not so. According to Naipaul:

The hippies of Western Europe and the United States appear to have done so; but they haven't. Out of security and mental lassitude, an intellectual anorexia, they simply cultivate squalor. And their calm can easily turn into panic. When the price of oil rises and economies tremble at home, they clean up and bolt. Theirs is a shallow narcissism; they break just at that point where the Hindu begins: the knowledge of the abyss.[28]

Naipaul's comments generalize over a broad spectrum of travelers and discount among them those who seek "the knowledge of the abyss." That is, in fact, what many of them were doing on the unfamiliar Asia road. And if some Western travelers bolt in panic, it may be not because they are disparaging but because they are discouraged and see a thing that is beyond them.

The key to understanding India, an elusive goal that frustrated many overland travelers and contributed to their general confoundment about the place, lies in its historical geography, and in comprehending how that history has absorbed, even welcomed, cultural invasions and infusions, to render still an essentially Indian, *Hindu*, essence. There one finds the basis for the extraordinary display of culture and traditions that mark for the traveler the soul of India: the ancient music of the ragas, the miniature paintings showing Maharashis on the hunt, ritual temple behavior that is based on the Vedic cosmology, stones cut with the erotic positions of the *Kama Sutra*, snake charmers, colorful costumes symbolizing the diverse cultures, and the extraordinary panorama of ordinary life that links the past with the present and the new travelers with the place.

In crossing from Lahore in Pakistan to Armritsar in northwestern India, the overland route dissolves into the vastness of the Indian landscape. As a culmination of the long Asia road, India was for many a disappointment—it failed to offer a final resolution to the journey, remained ambiguous and uncompleted, like a sentence without a period. It simply pointed in new directions. It failed to confirm the "Orient" as a singular place, as Said would allow, precisely because it contained the diversity of Asia—an almost incomprehensible subject. If India was disturbing for some travelers, it is because they were growing out of previously held concepts, but without having yet formed an unequivocal replacement to them; indeed, none would be forthcoming. This reinforced the ever-present tension on the journey between the intellectual baggage of the fantasy found and the fantasy sought.

The way into India for most Asia overlanders was first to New Delhi. As India's capital, the city provided the necessary administrative services—visas, special clearances, a mail drop, rail tickets. It also was a place to get acquainted with the country. That inevitably meant getting to know its past. Both old and New Delhi, with their contrasting ambiance—one spontaneous and colorful and the other deliberate and drab—merged into a sprawling urban landscape, and provided a good first glimpse at how ancient India became modern. The dazzling history of Delhi is presented to the tourist in an equally dazzling son et lumière production at the city's Red Fort, a 450-year-old reminder of the Moguls who, under the fifth emperor, Shah Jehan, controlled northern India in the sixteenth and seventeenth centuries.

One night as I watched the Red Fort production, brightly colored lights spotlighted the architecture of the fort and a spirited narrative in Hindi and English, with the accompanying sound effects of bird trills, clashing swords, and merry-makers, transported tourists to the Peacock Throne located in the Hall of Private Audience (the seat, itself, is of course in Iran) and to a time when Delhi was "the center of the universe." After the show the tourists around me—an international mix dominated by native Indians on vacation—applauded wildly. But it left vacant for me any visceral connection to the historical drama or to the place it meant to portray. The lights were nice, but I never sank into the thing.

Fortunately, the history of India is not restricted to the amusement park of the Red Fort, however compensatory that may be for some tourists. It is found most vividly instead in the twisted alleyways of the old city, in the bazaars and the silver emporiums of Chandi Chowk, in the countless tea shops and cheap curry stalls that line the back ways of the walled sector of Delhi. To walk those ancient lanes is to move from the enacted history of the Red Fort to the living history of the Indian street theater, from the son et lumière to *Salaam Bombay!*

A longer step into India's past could be had aboard a slow-moving mail train bound for one of that country's rural places. For most travelers, such a journey began first with a stop in Agra to glimpse the Taj Mahal. The ethereal beauty of that monument, "where the architect ends and the jeweler begins," hovering over the flat river plain, appears first as a distant ghost structure of white marble and minarets. It stopped me in my tracks. Upon closer examination, the detail of inlaid stonework, the gardens, and the exquisite symmetry of the lines of the building were revealed and affirmed in my imagination everything that I had been told about that place and about India.

The seventeenth-century Mogul emperor Shah Jehan laid the foundations for the Taj Mahal in 1631 and the monument was completed as a mausoleum to hold the sarcophagus of his wife Mumtaz Mahal. His design was to build an identical structure in black marble across the Jamuna River and to connect the two monuments by a silver bridge. Their complementary images, reflected on the placid surface of the river water, could then merge into one. Shah Jehan was deposed in 1658 by his sons and locked up in the Red Fort, and the second monument was never built. But today the majesty of the extant Taj Mahal rekindles travelers' worn spirits, precisely because it so clearly embodies the travelers' vision of India. In Mark Twain's words:

> You soon find your long-ago dreams of India rising in a sort of vague and luscious moonlight above the horizon-rim of your opaque consciousness, and softly lighting up a thousand forgotten details which were parts of a vision that had once been vivid to you when you were a boy, and steeped your spirit in the tales of the East.[29]

From Agra, the overland road totally lost its definition, blended into the Indian countryside along numerous arteries, and ferried travelers into the center of the subcontinent. Like R. K. Narayan's novels, India's heartland for travelers became a journey into the comedy of sadness. And like Narayan's fictional Malgudi, a village metaphor for all of India, the traveler's journey ranged across the wide material and spiritual landscapes of India. Minuscule against the sheer press of humanity in India, the Western travelers confronted an ironic solitude that derived from their place located on the outside of the moving panorama. They, like the cast of Malgudi characters in Narayan's novels, experienced the dislocating comic and tragic revelation that "in some stage of one's life one must uproot oneself from the accustomed surroundings and disappear so that others can continue in peace."[30]

Against this background—the patina of place and people and the trivial pursuits that are endlessly, but with exquisite fidelity, reproduced in Indian life such that they make up life itself—it is impossible to describe, without hyperbole or stereotype, India as a travel destination for the Asia overlanders. The country is too vast and the trajectories of the travelers too complex to summarize.

Key places however, shared a spot in their itineraries. Goa,

located on the southwest coast—the first Western foothold in South Asia—was known among the overland travelers as a wintering place where the beaches and oceans, the green hills, and exotic fruits combined to make it an easy and inviting place.[31] The Portuguese colonialists had created a European landscape in Goa that the overland travelers immediately responded to—a taste of home.

But where Goa meant self-indulgence, the holy city of Benares, located further to the east along the Ganges River and a second important stopover along the India road, was for self-sacrifice. It was a place where devout Hindus went to die and to burn their dead, to dump the ashes into the Ganges and let them swirl into the river's current and out of the Wheel of Samsara, to escape the trap of reincarnation. The travelers who visited Benares came to watch this spectacle, to immerse themselves not in the waters of the Ganges, which was filthy and polluted, but in the reverence there that was all around. Benares was steeped in the sensual mysteries of India and many overland travelers stayed merely as onlookers, voyeurs into the mystic chasm that forever separated them from the Indian people and the place around them. Between Agra and Goa, and Delhi and Benares, the countryside was as vast as the itineraries of those exploring it.

The Magic Buses, unequivocal in the barren deserts of central Asia, were lost in the color of India, but emerged again in the northern India state of Uttar Pradesh along the Himalayan border. The last grinding leg of the overland journey was uphill, from the border town of Birgunj through the middle mountains of the Kingdom of Nepal and then into the Kathmandu Valley, where Kipling found "the wildest dreams of kew" and where the Asia overlanders disembarked for the last time. To go further meant to go by foot, something only a few overlanders meant to do. Not when Kathmandu offered hotels at ridiculously cheap rates, hashish after meals in restaurants with the names of "Yin-Yang" and

"Nirvana," pie shops, temples, and used bookstores, all situated along a short thoroughfare called "Freak Street."

Today, at the outskirts of Kathmandu, near a new brick factory spewing pollution, is a vacant and weedy lot where old and abandoned vehicles are left. Nestled among the rusted frames of Indian lorries is the junked remnant of a Magic Bus. Its loud colors are dimmed somewhat from age, but the cracked windows are labeled still with legible city names: London, Amsterdam, Istanbul, Kabul, Delhi, Kathmandu. Points along the route. No one pays any attention to the bus. How it got there is a mystery, since most of those early vehicles found their way back to Europe. A few blocks from the auto junkyard is Freak Street. It is a burnt-out, grimy memory of its past, where a few aged hippies hang around looking for smoke, and where young urban Nepalis hustle the new tourists, those who come for a quick peek at the past, with forgotten slang and come-ons that are decades old.

Kathmandu now chokes in its polluted air and congested traffic. Each time I visit, I return to Freak Street, as forlorn as it is, in my attempt to momentarily lock into that earlier place. I meet a few others like myself, on a slow ramble down forgotten brick alleys, and I wonder whether they, too, had been there a long time ago. The tourists in Kathmandu have diffused through the city to refocus on a swanky section called Thamel. There the travelers of the 1990s meet, sleep, and eat in abundance. It is a busy part of the city, jammed with lodges, restaurants, and trekking agencies. Most of the Westerners who walk the streets of Thamel are tourists on a vacation, not travelers on a journey. They arrived in Kathmandu, not by way of overland aboard rusty buses and third-class trains, but by the agencies of the world adventure tourism industry. This year it is Nepal, next year it is the Amazon, or the East African savanna, or wherever their adventure tour will take them.

3

By All Means

"You are so fortunate, you get to see the world—"
Indeed, indeed, sirs, I have seen the world.
Spray splashes the portholes and vision blurs.
—DEREK WALCOTT, *THE FORTUNATE TRAVELLER*

The overland travelers who cross the world in their quests of the imagination follow the old explorers' routes to fashion new and highly personal journeys, focus their geographic visions in the light of new discoveries, and meander slowly across the distant landscapes with an eye close to the ground and a wish oftentimes to sink into a place, to be absorbed by it. They endure hardships en route, they *travail*—the epistemology of travel; the rewards of their journeys derive largely from the efforts they put into them. A certain loftiness accompanies the rigors of a journey. At day's end, under lingering desert twilights or against the alpenglow of snow summits, when conversation among travelers turns to reminiscence, it is the worries and the arduous times that are foremost recounted; all know that such ephemeral moments are shared by the others and will be understood by them—that is a bond of travel. Such people seek not to overcome the obstacles of geography that confound their paths but to absorb them, to claim them, and to be changed by them. The vagaries of climate, the clash of cultures, the conversation that emerges in bits and slices from silence or from animated gestures, the iconography of foreign landscapes comprehended, all compound until, as if a slowly unraveled cocoon, the journey metamorphoses the wayfarer and the real business of travel, that which links the inner and the outer worlds of the traveler, begins in earnest. Such a thing requires both a journey's history and its geography; it distinguishes between the travelers, who tarry, and the tourists, who move quickly over vast distances. The two thus are divided by time as well as space, and they therefore occupy vastly different worlds, following paths that may briefly intertwine in the most unlikely places, but which will never fuse.

The sense of urgency that may accompany such travel stems not only from the fact that many people seek places that are on the edge of extinction, for that is a provocation of travel, but because they seek the very experience of travel itself, before it also disappears. With the advancement of society, the faraway places lose their distance and, most important, their secrets. If nothing else, the traveler is an escapist, willing to go to the ends of the earth to flee the security that makes home so mundane and predictable. Yet everywhere we find that places are coming together, assimilating; the diffusion of Western society into the non-Western world attenuates the discord of humankind and that, coupled with the abandonment of the slower modes of passage, threatens the opportunities for classical travel in the modern age. The anthropologist Claude Lévi-Strauss knew this when he wrote:

> Journeys, those magic caskets full of dreamlike promises, will never again yield up their treasures untarnished. A proliferating and overexcited civilization has broken the silence of the seas once and for all. The perfumes of the tropics and the pristine freshness of human beings have been corrupted by a busyness with dubious implications, which mortifies our desires and dooms us to acquire only contaminated memories.[1]

Lévi-Strauss, without idealizing "natural man"—a common temptation of modern romantics—laments the possible fate not only of anthropologists but of all social humankind, and his concern extended to travelers as well when he wrote, "The first thing we see as we travel round the world is our own filth, thrown into the face of mankind."[2] In his wide travels as an anthropologist, Lévi-Strauss observed in the landscapes of the Third World the disturbing history of the Western world—worlds moving together and, as a result, places coming apart. But places contain their own identities as well, singular realms that do more than mimic the monoculture of the West.

I have visited many localities throughout the world that retain an exceptional character: narrow, twisted alleyways in Kathmandu where sacred cows steal vegetables from obliging vendors; the Saturday market in Oaxaca filled with Indian vendors and all imaginable goods; elaborate Jain temples carved in sandstone that soar skyward in Rajasthan; the thatched *fales* of Samoa, and the reefs of the Tokelau atolls where, at low tide, village pigs forage on the sea grasses and swim across tidal channels. I have wandered the aromatic medina in the tented center of Marrakech—Morocco's desert outpost—furrowed rice fields behind oxen during the wet summer monsoon in central India, and spent long winter days in Tibetan monasteries when chanting monks and howling winds were the only sounds I heard.

I have seen the bodies burn in the holy fires along the Ganges ghats in Benares; polo games played by horsemen on the plains of northern Afghanistan; sweet vendors in Pakistan and flower vendors in Bangkok; T'ai Chi Chuan practiced mornings by the elderly in the city parks of Hong Kong. I have eaten dog, pig, sour curds, sparrows, grasshoppers, and chicken feet; traveled by steamboat, bamboo raft, yak, horse, camel, and elephant. I have slept in goatskin tents with Bukharwal herders, adobe huts in the Thar desert, thatch huts on Pacific beaches, medieval castles, and caravansaries, and standing against a tree one long night in eastern Turkey in a driving rainstorm.

In this swarm of imagery and experience is an ordered world, defined by custom, accommodated by human choice, and resolved by my own subjectivity. It is a patchwork of places and people, real and fanciful, that is so diverse that it seems at first inconceivable that they could be much the same. Yet everywhere I find places on such a path toward conformity. Places that no longer stretch backward to connect with their pasts, but forward to greet the intrusions of the Western world—in which they perceive their futures to lie. Tourists, stretched along new inroads to greet the remote places, are among the early harbingers of such change.

The encroaching Western societies homogenize the traditional worlds, thereby removing much of the chance for the accidents of travel, the misadventures that make the adventures, and in which lie the metaphors of travel. Moreover, the travel experience itself, over the past several decades, has degraded to its commercial equivalent—tourism, and now new and major industrial efforts convey visitors to the most distant places on earth, where such people are called "adventure travelers"—as if they are something other than full-blown tourists, when they are not. Nonetheless, the prolific adventure tour brochures painfully argue that they provide something different from ordinary tourism, antithetical, even, to mass tourism. In a published letter to prospective clients of the Above the Clouds Trekking agency, Director Conlon stated:

> You have to get into an area that has not been exposed to tourism, because if the local people have the concept of tourism in their mindset, it may be impossible for them to treat you as anything but a tourist. And the agents who are designing your trip and/or leading you on the itinerary should be masters of the Art of Travel.[3]

The divide that is constructed between tourists and travelers in Conlon's adventure appeal is commonplace, and pointedly so, in the industry literature. Most of the adventure travel firms are led by persons who have had experiences along the overland travel road, or who spent considerable time as Peace Corps volunteers living in a Third World country, or from various expatriate positions maintained abroad. Such people have visited distant places as someone other than a tourist and most wish to continue to do so. Establishing an adventure travel agency allows that opportunity. Yet in establishing tours to remote adventure destinations located mainly in the Third World, the agencies promote experiences that they suspect may ultimately be unattainable under the conditions that are provided in the adventure packages. In the end, they are making a living.

Terrarium Tourism

With our sense of a shrinking world—a spatial condition brought on by technological improvements of global media and infrastructure, and by the constraints of diminished time—a relative and a real product of our own busyness, the prospects for the journeys of adventure and exploration that take us outside of our familiar worlds appear dimmed and more elusive than ever before. They are not, of course, but with more of us each year wishing to be led on adventures rather than to create our own, the edges of those unfamiliar worlds become blurred and are pushed further into the back of beyond.

Conventional tourism, that which brings us contrived experiences in places created precisely to hold them, persuades us that it can cut the sharper line of adventure travel as it pursues the products of its own creation. Over the past fifteen years, the tourism industry, by viewing adventure travel as a recent travel trend and a contemporary market demand, has designed entirely new tour packages that now make accessible for tourists some of the most geographically isolated places on earth. The agencies that specialize in the adventure tours now occupy a legitimate niche in the global tourism economy. Their efforts are coordinated by new institutions in the travel industry that were developed specifically to promote the adventure tourism alternatives.

In 1991, the first World Congress on Adventure Travel and Ecotourism was convened in Colorado Springs, Colorado; a second congress was held in 1992 in Whister, British Columbia; and a third occurred in Manaus, Brazil, in the autumn of 1993. The 1993 Adventure Travel Congress was the first to be held outside the Western economies of North America. Hosted by the Adventure Travel Society, the Amazonas Tourist Board (Emamtur), the Brazilian Institute for Tourism Development, and the United Nations Environment Program, it propitiously offered the Brazilian rain forest, one of the world's truly magnificent natural areas, as its venue. The rain forest is also the world's highest priority region for environmental conservation.

By locating the congress along the banks of the Amazon, the Adventure Travel Society explicitly located itself outside the conventions of Western tourism and implicitly transferred its interests to the Third World, where, in fact, most adventure tourism now occurs. In addition to a slate of keynote speeches and practical workshops on such topics as "Be Aware or Beware," "Paths of Progress," and "Going It Alone," the conference schedule provided numerous opportunities for day trips to nearby "ecolodges" and nature preserves—field trips meant to portray adventure tourism's *modus operandi in situ*. The field excursions included trips to EcoPark, where participants could "walk through the tropical forest where there is an abundance of animals living in the wild"; to the forest amphitheater at Natureza Camp to "experience first hand what you've only been reading about"; and to Ariau Jungle Lodge for "the only treetop lodge in the Amazon."[4] These meetings bring together tourism industry leaders and environmental experts to discuss the special issues of adventure travel, its relationship to the global economy, and its impacts on local natural environments and indigenous people. The formidable assumption behind much of this dialogue is that the new forms of adventure travel represent something different, that it therefore contrasts with the long-established conventional forms of tourism, not only in terms of where it leads visitors but in how it does so. Apart from a gratuitous sprinkling of academics and environmental luminaries, the congresses appear to be comprised mainly of government policy makers and tourism industry leaders who view adventure travel positively as the New Age market of what will become by the year 2000, according to the World Tourism Organization, the world's leading economic activity.

But the distinctions made by the tourism industry between adventure travel, or its cohort, ecotourism, and ordinary tourism escape me; the former seems to contain simply specialized segments of the latter. The term *ecotourism* strikes me as an oxymoron; its value as an ecological niche seems less apparent than its value as a market niche. The chief executive officer of the Walt Disney Company, a firm responsible for satisfying the most ambitious travel fantasies with floating resorts and theme parks constructed around the world, is a major advocate of "environmental and culturally sustainable" adventure travel; indeed, that person coined the term "soft adventure" to describe how tourism can provide safe versions of otherwise potentially dangerous adventures. But is he talking about new *adventure* theme parks? The Disneyland corporation is expert at promoting the visual consumption of manufactured versions of America's vernacular landscapes, but would it do so well in promoting places known precisely to be un-American?[5]

The prospect of nature parks becoming ecotourism theme parks is real. Such a thing already occurs widely with culture as the theme. For example, Hawaii's Polynesian Cultural Center presents the diverse peoples of the Pacific in a concrete terrarium of pseudo-villages and mock ceremonies. Any vestige of authenticity that the showcase may hold is obliterated by the production of just about every stereotype the Western imagination holds for the "South Seas." Tourists arrive at set times aboard luxury buses for a dinner buffet and culture show. Afterward they walk by planted palms and model thatch *fales* to the souvenir shops and photograph the costumed students who attend the nearby Brigham Young University and who work at the center in lieu of the university tuition.

The Polynesian Culture Center contributes little new learning, but it does reaffirm among visitors their latent imagery about South Pacific life. Most visitors leave the site quite satisfied, since little makes us feel better than when someone tells us that we are right about something that we know we are wrong about. The extension of similar artifices to the natural world appear to be imminent. Examples can already be seen in such places as Everglades City, Florida, with its swampboat tours and alligator wrestling. While full-blown terrarium tourism in the Third World may sustain the interests of small groups of elite tourists—the market for most ecotours—the burgeoning adventure tourism field would seem to explode the bounds of such constrained places.

Jerry Mallett, the current president of the Adventure Travel Society, writes in glowing words about the growth of adventure travel and the less-than-benign, spin-off benefits of the adventure industry—among others, the equipment and clothing industries:

> The leisure equipment industry has created markets where no one ever dreamed there was one. Cross-country skis, roller blades, inflatable rafts, scuba diving, climbing gear, back-packs, cameras, surfboards, kayaks and all unbelievable accessories. In order to look good when we get to the wild places, the clothing industry out-did itself. Swimsuits, wet suits, winter parkas, climbing pants, bicycle shorts, foot gear for all occasions and of course incredible colors![6]

The adventure travel industry has excelled also in creating new tourist places where "no one ever dreamed there was one": steamship tours along the Sepik River in Papua New Guinea, esoteric forays into tantric Buddhism amidst the windswept monasteries and the dzongs of Ladakh in northern India and Dolpo in Nepal, wildlife viewing in the Okavango Delta of Botswana, birding in the high canopies of Amazonia, tribal tours into the Golden Triangle, and many others. As Mallett exuberantly claims, "People have time and the equipment and they are learning about exotic places, peoples and events and they are on their way to see them."[7] That way, however, is determined for them by the adventure travel industry, promoted through its advertisements and meticulously planned to the last detail: "they," in other words, are on a tour.

Heroic Journeys

In a classical sense, exploration predates travel, which soon will be displaced fully by tourism. The distinctions between these remain troublesome, but the intermediary position of travel among them is more than temporal. Paul Fussell has written widely about travel and travel writers, and he noted that:

> All three make journeys, but the explorer seeks the undiscovered, the traveler that which has been discovered by the mind working in history, the tourist that which has been discovered by entrepreneurship and prepared for him by the arts of mass publicity.[8]

In a modern age when the possibilities for exploration appear to be gone, mainly because "undiscovered" places are rare today, explorers may be forced to change their cause as well as their methods, and consequently their raison d'être. As a Fellow of The Explorers Club, an international fraternity of perigrinators and fundraisers, I receive their quarterly magazine entitled *The Explorers Journal*, the contents of which comprise the published accounts of club member expeditions. The stories that appear in the pages of the journal are

full of cautious references to stone-age tribes and ancient rituals, to mountaineering exploits and spelunking—the last refuges—and to the endless personal rites of passage that mark the authors' experiences.

Each issue also contains "The President's Page." Here, the club's leader explains the role and conduct of the club and of its members. Such messages make it clear to the reader that explorers today should be scientists, not travelers; seekers of truth, not adventure; recipients of academic degrees, not knighthoods. Nicholas Sullivan, The Explorers Club president in 1990, explained that the club goals were "to encourage and sponsor exploration . . . it does not exist to sponsor adventures . . . an adventure is exploration gone wrong."[9]

Despite these proclamations, a quick read of *The Explorers Journal* will show that most writers, despite the admonitions of their club president, see in themselves the romance of adventure and discovery. In a review of the contents of recent issues of *The Explorers Journal*, I found articles with such titles as "Stone-Age Mysteries in Irian Jaya," "Camel Trekking with Sir Edmund Hillary," "The Hayes River Expedition: How to Turn a Kayak into Toothpicks," "The Mummified Bulls of Saqqara," and "The Untamed Masaii of Tanzania." Under the rubric of the scientific expeditions sponsored by The Explorers Club, we find a labyrinth of lost diggings in search of cultural wealth—scramblings for a new holy grail, camel caravans, and cave paintings, the quest for lost Incan forts and the mountains of the Jinn, penis gourds, treacherous kayak rivers, and deep-cave diving.

We find also the Annual Black Tie Dinner at The Explorers Club Hall in the Lowell Thomas Building in New York City, its tropical hardwood walls stained from decades of cigar smoke, a speaker's podium worn by a history of exploration's eloquent luminaries, and the club archives, which include expedition reports, charts, maps, diaries, letters, photographs, and other artifacts—an impressive collection of documents, memorabilia, and memoirs, caught under glass and dust. They underscore the notion that exploration without adventure is egregious. Unadmittedly, The Explorers Club exists to promote both of these in its fellowship of members. Indeed, the club associates are called Fellows to imply a sort of consortium—consorts, from the Latin *consors* meaning "one who shares the same fate." The club hearkens backward to a long history of expeditions that documents the West's progressive fascination with the "uncivilized places," and it links forward to new scientific undertakings that affirm our affair with imperial knowledge. But the vast intermediate terrain is filled with the drift and detritus of innumerable journeys. To deny the adventure of exploration is paradoxical and incongruous since all discovery contains unanticipated events. Indeed, they frame the journey and, despite planning to control them, determine its direction. It is even more difficult, and more to the point, to imagine *tourism* as exploration, as Christina Dodwell inadvertently does in her book *An Explorer's Handbook: An Unconventional Guide for Travelers to Remote Regions.* In addition to the chapters covering the basics of what to pack and how to set camp, the book's fourth chapter describes "tested exits from tight corners," where Dodwell explains with effrontery how not to offend local customs, how to handle bandits and being arrested as a spy, and what to do in the event of cannibals. Not to be alarmed, though, since Dodwell writes, "The likelihood of being harmed by cannibals is very small; I have encountered them several times and never felt threatened."[10] I'm not sure such words are as reassuring to the modern traveler as they are alluring, and I'm even less certain about which century she was writing. The solo adventures described by Dodwell are precisely those decried by The Explorers Club, yet the latter is enamored by the exploits of the former—such persons are toasted and roasted and honored at formal banquets. These apparent contradictions could all be quite confusing and entirely beside the issue were they not to hold a common point: exploration, however defined, need not trivialize adventure, for both seek in travel the myth of the hero. This remains, even if the lands of discovery change. The philosopher Joseph Campbell reminds us that:

> We have not even to risk the adventure alone, for the heroes of all time have gone before us. The labyrinth is thoroughly known. We have only to follow the thread of the hero path.[11]

To equate the world of the early explorers and the latter-day overland travelers with Campbell's "hero's path," an acceptable proposition since most of the overland travelers would agree that their journeys embody the element of myth-adventure, is not to say that the path is orderly or linear or well defined at all. Such journeys might, instead, be called templates—patterns constructed from narratives and shared stories that guide the modern travelers through the unfolding landscapes. Along such ways, the bypassed places are not unknown places in a geographic sense, but they do constitute the lands of new discovery for the wayfarers. Furthermore, as all the heroes show us, the true rewards of an adventure lie not in uncovering new places but in the awakening of the inner spirit. This possibility widens with travel because each new location *becomes* a new place every time it is experienced by someone new. The philosophers Hegel, Nietzsche, and Lefebvre tell us that, contrary to the concretized spaces of Descartes—the Cartesian world of geometric properties—our world is composed of relational spaces, places that arise from realized experiences. For most of us, this remains inside, contributing not to the satisfaction that once completed, a journey ends, but to the deeper yearning to continue along new travel routes.

When this is captured by the travel writers, a particularly significant work is produced; for example, the burdened consciousness of V. S. Naipaul, the luminosity of Conrad, or the skepticism of Paul Theroux—they reveal to us landscapes not only of the earth but of the mind. Always, the ultimate travel is inward, involving imagination and wonder as well as distance. Hence, while it may be argued that *outward* exploration—the discovery of earthly places unknown to humankind—is all but finished, kaput, in the sense of a literal geography concerned with the world's surface, all manner of possibilities remain for *inward* exploration; it is the parallel of travel—space collapses into time, the product of the journey becomes autobiographical, a memory.

In the book *Journey without Maps*, in which he traces his trek through Africa, Graham Greene wrote, "The need, of course, has always been felt, to go back and begin again."[12] In the last page of his book, after completing the journey, Greene admitted:

> It isn't that one wants to stay in Africa: I have no yearning for a mindless sensuality, even if it were to be found there: it is only that when one has appreciated such a beginning, its terrors as well as its placidity, the power as well as the gentleness, the pity for what we have done with ourselves is driven more forcibly home.[13]

The edge of travel begins by deconstructing our previously held, loosely fabricated images of places, it continues by establishing new and personal relationships to the places that we visit, and often it concludes by reshaping the place we left and our very notions of it. Such metaphorical journeys, linked to travel in a classical sense by Greene in his books, are not possible in the short run, nor can they be attained in the commercially programmed tours or in the sightseeing clichés that produce the tourism landscapes that we now find scattered around the world. Therefore, they remain inaccessible to mass tourism—literal tourism, which produces such landscapes.

Even the so-called adventure travel industry dilutes the spirit of travel as it establishes its own well-worn circuits and popular destinations. Many of the new guidebooks are no more than factual compilations of the packaged adventure tours that lead to remote world locations. For example, the *Adventure Travel Guide* lists thousands of tours arranged by 685 tour operators; these range from mountaineering expeditions that climb summits to scuba dives into shipwrecks. Other guides tailor tours along specific themes or to specific world regions. The possibilities apparently are endless, as evidenced in the continual creation of new adventure tour packages.

As the industry expands, the individual entrepreneurs strive to offer new tours and the adventure agency names become less than descriptive. Wilderness Travel, one of the world's leading adventure agencies, now offers indulgent trips aboard Caribbean yachts and to country inns, in addition to its rigorous treks through the heart of the Himalaya. Despite the plethora of tours now available, most of the adventure packages share central features—namely, worry-free planning and, since they are group tours, pleasant camaraderie. But the heroes of the mythical journeys, according to Campbell, knew better than to join a crowd:

> They thought that it would be a disgrace to go forth as a group. Each entered the forest at a point that he himself had chosen, where it was darkest and there was no path. If there is a path it is someone else's path and you are not on an adventure.[14]

Despite its bewildering guises under the various labels of ecotourism, alternative tourism, nature tourism, or *responsible* tourism, today's commercial adventure travel differs insignificantly from other mass tourism. Nor is adventure travel anything necessarily new. For example, "nature tourism" has its roots in the nineteenth century in North America when parklands were established near the large cities as recreation areas for the urban dwellers. They were large playgrounds for the recently affluent and were designed to serve the purposes of alleviating social ills in the cities and rekindling an appreciation of nature among city people.

In the early twentieth century, national parks were established in especially picturesque wilderness with a similar dual purpose.

These events occurred at about the same time when many persons saw that the wilderness areas of North America were quickly disappearing under agricultural, industrial, and urban developments. Farmland expansion into forests, resource extraction for processing and manufacturing items of culture, the spread of cities into suburbs, and new "edge cities" all point to the frontier ethic of land use in North America. The widespread modifications of North American landscapes that have occurred since early settlement times are not generally cataclysmic; rather they show continual or intermittent applications of technologies, land managements, and valuations that reflect the changing nature of U.S. culture. That such a culture also changes nature is obvious. Our conflicting ideas about nature are imbedded in our frustrated attempts to preserve it under the siege of consumerism. It is ironic that tourism, the very denouement of a consumer society, should be invested at last with the task of preserving much of the wilderness that remains around the world.

The impetus of modern nature tourism, that which focuses primarily on the Third World, is the knowledge that the last major wild places on earth are threatened by modernization and may soon disappear. Like its predecessors in North America, where recreation development was considered necessary, even analogous, to conservation, Third World nature tourism combines economics and ecology into a new identity that now produces the adventure tourism landscapes. These are more than nostalgic places, viewed in the light of the past. They encompass a bewildering complex of contemporary agendas: the subsistence needs of native people for whom such landscapes offer the possibilities of life, the developmental needs of national economies that view economic activities to be top priorities, the recreational needs of global tourists who seek out such places for the relief that they may provide. Prior to the onslaught of adventure travel, only small numbers of overland travelers divulged such remote spaces.

The adventure tours now march with certitude through even the most distant places on earth in their highly regimented assaults, and they take on rivers or mountains, monuments or resident cultures, with tight itineraries and along precision routes. The tours have all the economy of a well-disciplined task force, and they carry with them their own sense of urgency—one that situates the conquered destinations among others of life's rare achievements, premier *accomplishments*, but which contain also the requisite witnesses to make the attainment public knowledge, a testimonial.

Such efforts connect to a history of tourism that links the Renaissance period with the grand tours of Europe, and it developed rapidly in the mid-nineteenth century under such entrepreneurs as Thomas Cooke, who made travel to distant places desirable for wealthy people by making it less irksome and more predictable. The modern adventure travelers, who today extend tourism's reach into the world's most inaccessible places, have behind them such a history and all the logical and logistical support the world tourism industry can muster.

Commercial adventure tourism promotes excursions to the world's tropical rain forests, the deserts, and the mountains, and incursions among the gorilla habitats, the cultural monuments, and the villages of the Third World—a plethora of "peripheral" places. But it is simply old tourism that at best covers new ground. The fact that the people who participate in it travel to distant places and to foreign cultures—the camps of the "other"—does not deny the fact that they are on a holiday. The task of the journey, indeed, the very design of the details, is for them not to worry. Instead, it preoccupies the professional tour arrangers who pride themselves on their abilities to *anticipate unforeseen events* and diffuse them, as one might disarm live ordnance, or remove them altogether from the journey as one might sweep the leaves that clutter a path and give it an undesirable look.

The adventure travelers on the commercial journeys trade

mystery for security and in the bargain they lose that which they seek. It's a double knot. Paul Bowles wrote in his book *Their Heads Are Green and Their Hands Are Blue*, "Security is a false god; begin making sacrifices to it and you are lost."[15] The first sacrifice adventure travelers make for security is adventure. Travel reservations, hotel check-ins, guides, fixed itineraries—all these compose the adventure travel experience and are meant to eliminate the element of surprise. Even the adventure destinations themselves can quickly become pseudo-places once they appear *exactly as they were imagined to be* or, more to the point, as they were advertised in the adventure publications. When the secrets are spilled before the journey, the actual tour becomes a shadow play.

In various places and situations, I have been mostly a traveler and occasionally a tourist. At no time, however, have I felt more unease than when I was led as a client on a commercial adventure tour, and told I was a traveler, when I knew I was a tourist. Although my purpose in joining the commercial tours has been largely critical, I cannot imagine how I could have felt *attached* to the experience, given the play of the journeys.

Cannibal Tours in Thailand

In 1990, I joined an adventure travel program in northern Thailand. Our group was to be led by jeep, boat, foot, and elephant for several days through the jungle and tribal villages located among the hills that spill across the northern stretches of that country. Rugged limestone formations, exquisite caverns made into Buddhist shrines, rough waterways, and mottled green tracts of pristine or degraded forest describe much of the physical landscape of Thailand's northern mountains. Dispersed throughout the region are several settlements of northern Thailand's hill tribes—the Karen, Hmong, Mien, Lahu, Akha, and Lisu peoples. They populate remote villages, live in houses made of thatch and bamboo, clear garden plots in the forest to plant rice and vegetables, grow opium on the hillsides for use as medicine and as a source of cash income, and keep pigs and chickens in courtyard stalls for meat. Handicrafts made in the villages—woven baskets, silver jewelry, and woodcarvings, together with local religion, elaborate costumes, and clan politics, distinguish the cultures that compose the complex of hill tribes. They add also to the village economies. The traditions and the lifestyles of Thailand's hill tribes, kept alive by the faith and the practice of people who have lived for centuries in the northern hills, now contribute to local wealth as they have become tourist commodities. The tourist treks into the hill tribe regions are sometimes billed as "cultural tours," other times as "nature tours," but always they combine elements of both against a backdrop of consumption—handicrafts, staged culture, and scenic views.

I was along on the trek to collect information about the tour, a voyeur into the lives of the tourists and, in fact, into the very life of the tour itself. But I wanted also to see for myself the northern hills and the people who lived among them. That desire leveled the field and made me a regular member of the tour, a *tourist*. Five of us in all—Europeans but for myself—signed on for the trek, with the addition of our guide and the errand-boys who would join us later in the journey. I had arranged for the tour in Bangkok with the local subsidiary of a somewhat obscure European adventure tour agency.

Like most such operations, the in-country office did much of the work—from greeting clients upon their initial arrival to arranging all local logistical efforts to guiding the actual tour. Unless arrangements were made within the host country, such as I had done, the payments were received at the agency headquarters located abroad. The vast distances that separate the offices and the paltry flow of funds that generally occurs between them ensures, as I was to discover, that considerable discrepancies occur between the advertised and the actual tour. From Bangkok our group was to proceed north by minivan to Thailand's second-largest city, the frontier town of Chiang Mai, which is located in a valley near the trekking regions and is the most convenient point of entry into the nearby highlands. For the sake of expediency, our itinerary called for night travel north from Bangkok. That meant that the little we might see of the most of Thailand would be obscured by darkness.

A few days before the group's scheduled departure from Bangkok, I arranged my own travel to Chiang Mai aboard a public bus. I wanted to stop en route at Sukhothai—an important political center of Siam before it was ravaged by Burmese invaders in the mid-eighteenth century. My northward journey carried me across Thailand's lush central plains, grain-golden fields interspersed by distant green thickets of coconut palms overtowering colorful frame homes, roadsides filled with bicyclists, the omnipresent canals jammed with waterboats, and everywhere flowers and temples. My stop in Sukhothai provided me with a sense of Thailand that in Bangkok was lost to the traffic, to the city noise and smog, and to the pervasive Westernization that marks Bangkok as one of Asia's most prosperous cities. Among the ruins at Sukhothai, I found a certain peace that I thought must surely describe Thailand's ancient Buddhist cultures.

As impressive as the monuments were—the delicate sculptures of Buddha figures and ancient kings, and the massive Wat Mahathat that was constructed by King Sri Indraditya in the early thirteenth century to be the magical center of his kingdom, it was the quiet of history and the morning coolness, the solitude before the vendors and other tourists arrived, that pleased me most about Sukhothai. Sitting among crumbling pagodas under the fragrant blossoms of plumeria trees, I could well imagine a time when instead of ruins the place was a lavish Buddhist state, when King Ramkhamhaeng ruled with paternal benevolence over a land that teemed with activity, a place described in his own writing:

> In the time of King Ramkhamhaeng this land of Sukhothai is thriving. There is fish in the water and rice in the fields. The lord of the realm does not levy toll on his subjects for travel-ling the roads; they lead their cattle to trade or ride their

horses to sell; whoever wants to trade in elephants, does so; whoever wants to trade in horses, does so; whoever wants to trade in silver and gold, does so.[16]

I should have lost myself to history in that place, but I was on a tour, and I couldn't linger or my party might leave me in Chiang Mai, the renowned "flower of the north," and I would then miss my trek to the hill tribe villages. In hindsight, I wish I had indulged myself at Sukhothai and missed the journey that followed.

The trails to the lost valleys of Thailand's famous Golden Triangle begin in Chiang Mai at a rowdy row of travel agencies (splashy signboards announce their special tribal tours) set amidst the insistent whine of the three-wheeled *thuk-thuks* and against the green backdrop of Doi Suthep. From the large number of tourist shops and travel agencies located in Chiang Mai, I supposed that our little group would not be trekking alone on the nearby mountain trails. Our travel into the hills began with a bus ride north from Chiang Mai past Chiang Dao and on to the smugglers' town of Fang, located at the Burmese border. I thought it odd and rather inauspicious that our trek through the fabled hills should begin in such a place, known mainly for the fact that each year enormous quantities of contraband opium passed the border here, attracting with its lure of wealth a rather dismal community bent on gaining riches quickly.

In Fang, we met our guide, a young lad behind Rebo sunglasses, wearing jeans and a Metallica T-shirt, who was to lead us on our solemn trek to the ancient Mien (Yao) villages of his birth. The Mien had migrated to this area from southern China about two millennia ago and, like so many of their ethnic neighbors living elsewhere in Thailand and in the bordering states of Burma and Laos, they had managed to retain in these remote hill lands much of their traditional lifestyle. That fact is the source of their tourist wealth. People visit from throughout the Western world to witness village life here. Of all the varied fascinations that the northern

tribal people hold for Westerners, their ceremonies, costumes, and handicrafts, I found most intriguing the fact that they are shifting cultivators, slash and burn farmers, swidden gardeners.

Horticulturists really, Thailand's hill people live intimately with the jungle by clearing small parcels of it, cutting and burning the slash to release the nitrogen that in the tropical forests is stored in the vegetation and to transfer it to the impoverished soil, where a complex of layered crops are planted in a style that mimics the forest structure. Every three years or so, after the soil is depleted of its short-lived fertility, the farmers move onto another parcel, cut and burn it, plant, and then move onto another plot, repeating the process several times until the first cleared plot revegetates— allowing approximately twenty years of fallow period—when it can be rotated again into the slash and burn cycle. Such an elaborate method of farming is common in the tropics.

Under conditions of low population density and where adequate forest land is available, shifting cultivation is quite sustainable. Today in Thailand, where extensive forest clearing and high population densities describe much of the northern hill lands, the shifting cultivators together with the timber cutters, cattlemen, and the other forest users are degrading the country's tropical forests and the soils beneath them at an alarming rate. I wanted to see where that happened. Where other tourists might take postcard pictures, I sought visible destruction: burnt fields and cleared slopes, eroded gullies. While my companions might examine handwoven baskets and embroidered cloth, I looked for digging sticks and hunting gear, and imagined them being used.

I thought that my village trek would provide me with such views, but after traveling with the group for a short while I was proved wrong. Two of my companions were interested only in reaching the first rest village, where they could acquire some opium and smoke it. The other tour members wished to procure handicrafts. They had no difficulty en route since everyone we met had something to sell, confirming my doubts that we were breaking virgin tourist ground here—despite the adventure tour brochure announcing "remote, untouched tribes." My bargain-hunting companions squealed in delight whenever an especially fine piece of handiwork was obtained. All the members of our group, myself included, continually jockeyed to photograph the ordinary postures of people living in the bypassed villages. That too, carried a cost—a dime approximately for each shutter click (the geographer Phil Deardon estimated that posing for photographs brings an estimated $5,800 per year into the northern Thai village economies).[17]

I was both impressed and appalled with how completely each transaction our group had with the villagers was reduced to its monetary equivalent. I have seen this before in many places—the commodification of life, but in few places had it assumed the art form that I saw here on the tourist trails of northern Thailand. It appeared to me that *everything* here was for sale. In the late morning our guide struck up a conversation that told me so. He wished to know if I wanted a village girl for the night, since we would stay at a tribal home. To the best of my recollection, our sprightly conversation, on a path at the outskirts of a Yeo village, went like this:

"You alone?" he asked, knowing full well I was.

"Yes," I replied.

"Wanna girl?" he asked, glancing around furtively as if we might be overheard, knowing that we would not, and that no one would care.

"What's that?" I replied, knowing full well what he meant.

"You know, wanna nice village girl for tonight? Young one," he added, as if that would explain it, giggling and gesturing in a universally obscene manner.

"No, thanks," I responded.

He shrugged, a bit surprised, and walked off.

Sex tourism is big business in Thailand. While courtesans, concubines, and brothels have operated for centuries in the country for a male Thai clientele, the promotion of prostitution for tourism purposes dates to the Vietnam War, when the United States military made it a common practice to take holidays from the war among the brothels and bars of Bangkok. After the war the Pentagon trade dropped, but the number of tourists to Thailand increased, from just over 0.5 million in 1970 to 2.8 million in 1986. With almost 90 percent of the tourists in Bangkok being European men, it is clear that sex tours remain popular.

The bawdiness of Bangkok's bar district has been notably absent in the north, even if sex itself is for sale. The northern areas have a different image, intended to provide a unique appeal for tourists in Thailand. The Tourism Authority of Thailand, which in other instances promotes an image of modernity for the country, describes the northern tribes as "simple and unspoiled." The sociologist Eric Cohen described the Western tourists who visit them as interested in culture and respectful of local customs.[18] Dearden described the Westerners who trek in Thailand as young and educated, and in search of "authenticity." While all that may be so, it seems to me, based on my limited experience with one commercial tour, that eroticism has been uniquely incorporated into the tribal treks. And it is not limited to sex.

Some of my companions had no difficulty finding opium at the first village we visited. Apparently, quite a few trekking tourists smoke it (Dearden estimates the number at 40 percent), and villagers proffered it immediately when our group passed through their place. Most tourist usage, however, is restricted to the preemptory stops at the village headman's house, where the tours are obliged to pay a fee and where the drug is often sold. The unrefined opium used and sold in the villages is derived from the poppy flower, an extraordinary plant, seen in sweeps across the hill slopes, that splashes the green jungle with luxurious colors. Equally intoxicating are the resins of the plant. These are gathered by cutting short slits into the seed pods, allowing the sap to escape through the incisions and congeal on the outer surfaces of the plant, where they are scraped with the curved blade of a specially made opium knife. This is done in the early morning when the cool air hardens the sticky resin. The black and gooey product is then pressed for storage into small balls which look much like rabbit pellets.

For smoking, the opium balls are carefully placed into a black and silver opium pipe (a prized handicraft sold in many of the tourist villages) and then lighted over small lamp fires. While opium is widely used in the region as an herbal drug, few tribe members smoke it to addiction. Most villagers agree, however, that it is good business for the tourists (Dearden estimated that opium sales generate annual revenues of $110,400 for the northern villages). While the contradictions of opium use among the tourists are apparent, it was equally obvious to me that smoking opium was just another adventure, not a mounting addiction, for the adventure travelers.

With all the distractions offered at the beginning of the tour, I saw little of the countryside through which we passed. Therefore, in the afternoon hours of that first day, until dusk when we stopped for the night, I paid extra attention to the land along our route. I was rewarded by a foreground view of scrubland and scattered garden plots, occasionally interspersed with fairly dense stands of what looked like virgin forest, and a backdrop of distant vistas showing scarred hills. The trails were well used and hardpan from the dry weather; on this section of our tour we were afoot, but the next day we would travel by elephant. Occasionally our guide led us along ridgelines where we enjoyed panoramic sweeps of a rolling country-side capped by limestone cliffs and cut by deep river gorges. It is quite an extraordinary landscape, and I enjoyed the leisurely pace that our group maintained. My silent reveries across the distant landscapes were obtained only in brief gazes, however, interrupted by continual outbursts from the other members of our tour, exclamations of delight or, alternatively, complaints.

The tour, for me, was a mistake. The conflicting abilities and interests of the tour participants prevented us from acquiring any steady rhythm to our walk and this prohibited the chance to individually connect with the land through which we were traversing. The journey had all the explorative qualities of a zoo tour, and it was just about as demeaning as that when we entered into the neat trailside villages. Promoted as a "cultural tour," our hill tribe trek was little more than ethnic voyeurism. My interest in the trek quickly waned as I learned that what was advertised as "adventure travel" simply turned out to be gang tourism, cannibal tourists in a foreign land.

My shame in participating in it was reinforced later that night when our group lodged at the house of the village headman. He apparently had made arrangements to accommodate all the tours that passed through his village. This made him quite a lot of money, although he was hardly a gracious host, but it made him also the envy of the other villagers, a condition long imposed by his political stature in the village but now reinforced by his newfound tourism wealth.

The details of that evening several years ago now seem trivial, but had I been a "real" tourist at that time, I would have complained immediately about the stink, the dirt, and the lack of mosquito netting. I did not because it struck me as possible that this aspect of the tour was most likely the only thing about it that approximated the "real thing." Besides, my tour companions complained loudly enough for the entire group. Before long, despite the languor of opium, they verbally assaulted not only our guide, who had made arrangements favorable to himself without the knowledge of his boss in Bangkok, but also the village chief, who apparently was in cahoots with our guide.

It became apparent that no prior arrangements had in fact been made in that village for our tour. The money was gone. Tempers flared. After an hour of pleas and impassioned discussion, during which our guide switched sides incessantly, everyone agreed before fisticuffs occurred that it would be best to return in the morning to Fang three days early and then make the journey back to Chiang Mai. Call it quits. After a sleepless night for me (my companions slept well), our little group hit the back trail and reached Fang in record short time. I dropped from the group there and arranged my own return to Chiang Mai: Good-by; wasn't it a nice time?

I located a space in the back of a Toyota pickup bound for Chiang Rai roundabout by way of a little-used dirt track. We headed east through sparsely settled jungle before tumbling down to the valley below us. The trip was slow and tedious, the road rutted and muddy, until we reached the escarpment above Chiang Rai. On the last ten downhill miles we lost the use of our brakes and the driver managed the curves by downshifting to slow the vehicle. I hopped off the gliding truck at the outskirts of town, shaken and sore and in search of clean hotel. The best that I could find was a small inn run by an Afghan hashish smuggler. The only other guest of the hotel was a German man who had been in a motorcycle accident several weeks before and was now recuperating. After one night in Chiang Rai, I took a bus to nearby Chiang Saen, a small trading town on the riverbank, where I looked onto the Mekong River and across to the apex of the Golden Triangle—that place where the borders of Burma, Thailand, and Laos meet. It was a splendid sight, awash in a clear mountain light; it rewarded me for the last miserable days.

Tactics of Adventure Tourism

My limited experience with adventure tourism in Thailand deflated some of the ideas I had held about the promise of such alternative tourism. Conversations with many other people tell me that my experiences were not unique. I found little in the tour to be alternative except the destination and even that was quickly becoming less so as such places receive more visitors each year. I discovered instead a tour that was more commerce than adventure, ungainly in its movements, and in the end an embarrassment. It may be reasonable to presume that had I chosen a better outfit, or had I gone to a different region, my adventure travel experiences in northern Thailand might well have been quite different.

I know from other experiences elsewhere, in Nepal for example and in the South Pacific, that it is quite possible for adventure tourism to succeed in delivering much of what it promises. But how often that is the case and at what cost remain for me troublesome questions. Elsewhere in Thailand, examples show how nature-based tourism can help local people economically while preserving environmental quality. For example, near Khao Yai National Park, local communities blend tourism with conservation and with agricultural diversification to reduce pressures on the thirty-year-old park—Thailand's first tropical rain-forest preserve that now encompasses 1,226 square miles.

At other locations in the country, especially in the northern tribal territories, where tourism is more fully developed and the numbers of tourists are high, the role of adventure tourism remains unclear. The notion of "authentic experiences" is important for adventure travel clients, and the environmental as well as economic consequences of such tourism for the host places are fundamental concerns for adventure travel; the former drives the industry and the latter shape it. Such questions are especially deserving since adventure travel has become one of the fastest growing sectors of international tourism and will undoubtedly shape the futures of many of the world's most geographically remote places.

The adventure travel industry, through its various agencies and publications, leads visitors into what are described as exotic and unknown places, unique cultural and natural settings, located mainly in the developing world regions. An inevitable collision of worlds results. Western adventure travel extends the geographical centers of international tourism to some of the most pristine places on earth. It thereby transfers the concerns of sustainable development to the world's foremost periphery. In this way, adventure travel is both a logical extension of the earlier overland travel experiences and a spearhead for new advances of mass tourism. These concerns seem to be lost on many of the practitioners of adventure travel, persons who look upon such trends with a certain glee and who see them as a sign of future economic opportunities.

The growth predicted for adventure travel is heralded by the many new tourism guides that emphasize adventure, the outdoors, and out-of-the-way places. Such established publishers as Sierra Club Books and St. Martin's Press publish several new outdoor travel guides annually, and they are joined each year by dozens of new titles from numerous smaller presses, including Wilderness Press, Globe Pequoit, John Muir Publications, Mountaineers Books, and others. The range of material provided by the hundreds of new books suggests that one person's leisure may well be another's adventure. They point to the reshaping of tourism and its new focus away from the common resorts and toward the formerly hidden places. Indeed the guidebooks themselves sharpen the focus of tourism as they point out places off the beaten track.

The edge of this alternative movement, that which preoccupies adventure travel in the Third World, cuts into the very frontier of world development, and in so doing it either steers a collision course to ruin for distant places and cultures or it imagines wholly new ways of sensitively visiting such places. In determining which will be the case, it is not so much the idea of adventure travel that is paramount, but rather its practice.

In a 1993 publication of the Washington, D.C.–based U.S. Travel Data Center, Jerry Mallet, of the Adventure Travel Society, identified the economic outlook for adventure travel as excellent. He predicted that active outdoor recreation will increase and noted that every country in the world is now targeting the adventure travel market. Moreover, he stated in his report that:

In just a few short years, adventure travel has grown tremen-
dously into the product that everyone wants. Over the past
few years, the travel industry, airlines and the hotels were
caught off guard when the leisure traveling public suddenly
wanted to go hiking, diving, river running, mountain biking,
birding, and visiting Mayan ruins and other archaeological
sites.[19]

Such a jubilant vision conjures lurid images of a not-so-stealthy
military assault. A page later in the same report, Mallett attributes
the growth of worldwide adventure travel partly to the proliferation
of inexpensive war surplus equipment converted to recreational
purposes:

Items such as rubber boats became river running tools, Jeeps
were the forerunner of the four wheel drive industry. Backpacks, cold weather gear, unfired $7 dollar Springfield 30-06
rifles and new materials that would become wind boards,
roller blades, mountain bikes, scuba equipment, kayaks,
hot air balloons and down jackets became inexpensive and
available.[20]

The terms commonly used by the adventure travel industry to
promote its activities—such phrases as "penetrating the frontier,"
"tracking," "fitness," "exciting and exhilarating," "challenging"—
assume the lexicon of a tactical strike, and it may only be proper that
they deploy the equipment designed by the Western military to
accomplish it. Yet counter phrases appear just as frequently in the
adventure travel promotions, terms such as "cultural respect,"
"privilege," "environmental protection," that suggest for modern
commercial adventure travel an alternate agenda that is more
ambivalent and somewhat schizophrenic beside the churlish call for
adventure.

Such inconsistencies derive from adventure travel's curious

blend of bravado and sensitivity, and they induce the notion that it is entirely feasible "to travel to remote destinations and still enjoy *the good life* [emphasis in original]."[21] Such statements, prolific among adventure tourism's promotional literature, imply that geography alone, without the material support provided by the new tour arrangers, precludes a good life. Part of the paradox of adventure travel stems from the fact that adventure travelers wish to immerse themselves in distant places in a rather comfortable way, but the places they visit attract them precisely because of the lack of amenities. Hence, the adventure travel packages offered by many travel agencies strive for a balance between comfort and experience such that they promote "a style *appropriate* to your adventure: *we never try to insulate you from a destination, just to enhance your overall experience* [emphasis in original]."[22]

Try as they may, however, the product of most adventure agencies is less a travel experience and more a tour; consequently, by most definitions, the modern adventurers who subscribe to one of the many thousands of adventure vacations offered each year are not travelers but tourists. Semantic differences aside, the implications of the one over the other are not lost on the adventure travel industry. Rarely, in fact, does one encounter among the adventure travel brochures the word *tourist*. It is more than a matter of editing, since the term has connotations that are antithetical to the goals of adventure travel, which explicitly are to outdistance the tourists and move beyond them in terms of both geography and experience.

At certain places in the world, the traveler and the tourist collide—often an embarrassment for both. This frequently occurs when tourist sites coincide with nodes forged along the overland travel circuits, where both groups share space, if not experiences or economies. For example, in the highlands of southern Mexico lies the rugged state of Oaxaca. It has long been a key point on the itinerary of the overland travelers along the "Gringo Trail," and recently Oaxaca has gained popularity for North American tourists who visit the ruins at Monte Albán and ply the beaches at Puerto Escondido.

In the center of Oaxaca City is the *zócalo*, a large brick and garden plaza built by the Spaniards with bandstands, cafés, and wrought iron benches, all shaded by purple flowering *jacaranda* trees. It is a gathering place mainly for Oaxaqueños—residents of the city drawn together by the geometry and the society of their city, but it also is where tourists visit, to photograph the churches and to dine at restaurants, and it is where travelers alight, to sip cups of coffee in sidewalk cafés. The peculiar interaction of the tourists and the travelers is primarily one of avoidance. In the gaze of the latter, the former are bourgeois, while tourists see travelers as insignificant. Neither wishes to be the other; both believe that they are something different.

The adventure tour industry plays this division to its economic benefit, fleecing the perceptions of prospective clients and haughtily describing how their paid clients are not tourists. But the fact is that such people *are* tourists, guided into new lands not by a literature of travel narratives or by their own private imaginations, but by the commercial efforts of the modern adventure tour agencies. Their guides are not the accounts of ancient explorers or even the contemporary alternative travel guidebooks; instead, such tourists rely almost exclusively on the lavishly illustrated, hyperbolic catalogues published by hundreds of adventure travel agencies that vividly portray images of "exotic" worlds, but provide little factual information about them. Such guided imagery promotes journeys fabricated not by experience but by commerce, wherein the travel narrative is displaced by advertising slogans.

All travelers impress themselves upon the places they visit, just as the cherished visas imprint their passports, transforming landscapes into commodities. This act is the covenant—the primal bond, to make use of Jamake Highwater's term, that tourism establishes with those primitive places that host it. It is first evidenced in the adventure catalogues which so artfully and pro-vocatively *sell* the places they describe. From selected photographs, other icons, and a capsule text, destinations are offered in a menu of exotic places for the discriminating tourist. For many modern Western tourists, driven by economy and pleasure and by a shallow image of the places they visit, the commodification of travel destinations is accepted without question, something to be ex-pected, rarely even mentioned. For the adventure travelers among them, propelled along alternative paths to seek a more durable experience of a place—and hence to potentially impress themselves more indelibly upon it, such an idea may seem sacrilegious, reprobate, or at least counter to the aims of travel. Yet it is so.

Even the circuity of travel forged in the overland journeys into Asia and to other world places, journeys that link backward to European world dominion and forward into the imagination, shapes new futures for distant places and alternate destinies for the people who inhabit them. Those innumerable quests of discovery that lay at the heart of Asia overland travel were long and drawn-out affairs. But overall, the numbers of such travelers remained low when compared to global tourism as a whole, and, while travel itineraries certainly were formed, such journeys dispersed travelers across a wide and uncertain landscape. Those journeys and the travel routes they produced reflect the ambitions of the early explorers who initially shaped them and, by telling the tale of the journey, the overlanders who continuously refashion them. In such a way, overland travelers were both following and creating the travel route, its geography, and the experiences that lay along the way. Robert Harbison, in his book *Eccentric Spaces*, describes the nature of such journeys in this way:

> Itineraries are imaginary constructions, often even historical
> reconstructions in which we follow the routes that are no
> longer there, visiting the thriving centers of the fifteenth cen-

tury, moving on lines of force that exist now only in the imagination, outworn forms remembered.[23]

The contemporary adventure travelers who pay large sums of money to join the commercial itineraries to places advertised as exotic differ from the overland travelers and the early explorers mainly by the fact that they undertake no critical role in creating the journey; the travel industry, instead, has assumed that task. Moreover, the tide of such modern adventurers spilling over the edges of the earth is larger and more powerful than ever before, with consequences not yet fully imagined. As consumers of tours, the modern adventurers may be distinguished from other tourists by nothing more than their Gore-Tex baggage and the destinations to which they aspire. Yet this separateness is important enough, precisely because of its geography and the fact that so little is known about the consequences of this new form of tourism.

In some of the most remote places on earth, the claims of large groups of adventure tourists over the land compete with the imaginative journeys of the overland travelers, as well as with the daily lives of native people for whom such places contain their identities. In places turned over to tourism, such conflicting claims often are adjudicated by economic developers who consciously, if not with conscience, select the forms of tourism that will prevail.

The economy of tourism may well contain elements of cultural conservation—the maintenance of cultural traditions and self-determinism. But when native places become tourism marketplaces, when costumes become curios, and when ceremonies are staged for the curious visitors, then the rights of local people over their land and even their culture are threatened. In a slow and inexorable way, indigenous people become distanced from their land, which may eventually result in the loss of ways of living—cultural genocide. The concern of the adventure travel industry about such things is incipient at best, and it manipulates the goals of biological and cultural diversity with the preservation of places for tourism gain.

The new adventure travelers appear driven less by wanderlust, the hallmark of the early explorers as well as the more recent overlanders, and more by the angst of knowing their middle age but not how they got there. They have money, evidenced by the exorbitant costs attached to the adventure tours, but little time. Banana Republic safari wear, L. L. Bean footgear, and Indiana Jones complexes may profile many such adventure tourists, but their fantasies are fueled by the hundreds of agencies worldwide that specialize in adventure tour packages. A 1992 article in the *New York Times* suggests that the tourist call of the wild has become an image harvest, with the "proliferation of packaged adventure tours bearing names like 'Everest Escapade' and 'Mystical Mustang,' titles right out of the Hardy Boys."[24]

The well-established adventure firms, such outfits as Mountain Travel, Wilderness Travel, Backroads, and Overseas Adventure Travel, produce lavish annual catalogues that describe in color photographs and flowery text the itineraries of their adventure expeditions. In those descriptions lie the lure of the places where the modern adventurers now go—gorilla watching in Rwanda, guerrilla watching in Nicaragua, monastic tours of Tibet (which highlight the destruction of its temples as well as the traditions that endure among them), river travel and spirit houses in Papua New Guinea, trekking in the high Himalaya, tracking in Kenya, and so forth.

The adventure catalogues replace the old travel literature and the alternative guidebooks, sources of inspiration and practical information for overlanders, with the brief, highly polished profiles of exotic destinations that show, in addition to the carefully edited production of places, *how well the client will be taken care of* en route. For the adventure tourism industry, adventure need not exclude comfort or safety. In fact, it is just this combination that appeals to adventure travel's rapidly growing clientele. Where such travelers go and the kinds of experiences they encounter are questions of geography. While the adventure traveler may not be concerned that "if it's Tuesday, this must be Belgium," they are fully cognizant of the fact that the tour they select should take them into unknown worlds, where perhaps even time itself stands still. But can the gestalt of travel, that conceptual leap that often occurs among people individually immersed in the experiences of a journey and a new place, be packaged?

Grand Tours to Lost Worlds

While the overland travelers aimed to write the script as well as to act the journey, the modern commercial adventure tourists are largely content with filling supporting roles, and they bring to travel a cast of characters straight out of the "Grand Days of Travel." In the new grand tours, yaks and llamas replace luxury liners and furnished Pullman coaches, camp tents serve as polished hotels, and local tribespeople wearing traditional cloth are the servants to the tourists. The marketing of the packaged adventure tours relies on the fact that they provide hassle-free experiences at remote locations in relative comfort. That is the main point of the tours; indeed it is the *only* point since, without it, the tourists would be travelers and in no need of such services.

The packages are designed for consumers who have little time to waste on the details of travel; which is to say that they want to quickly reach the viewpoints, the scenic overlooks, the adventure experiences, click a few rolls of film, perhaps take a spill for the thrill, and return home safe, sound, and on time. But without the details of travel, those matters which forge the journeys, the modern adventure travelers trade speed for the spirit of adventure and forsake serendipity for a steady schedule. Considering the large numbers of clients available for the adventure packages—hundreds of thousands each year—the exchange for many must be a bargain.

The commercial adventure travelers descend from an exalted lineage, not of itinerant explorers—the light of contemporary overlanders—but more properly of the aristocratic members of eighteenth-century Europe's "Grand Tour," albeit traveling in a more speedy fashion. Of the latter, Josiah Tucker, rector of St. Stephen's in Bristol, England, in a 1757 pamphlet entitled "Instructions for Travelers," wrote:

> Persons who propose to themselves a scheme for travelling, generally do it with a view to obtain one or more of the following ends, *viz. First*, To make curious collections as natural philosophers, virtuosos, or antiquarians. *Secondly*, to improve in painting, statuary, architecture, and music. *Thirdly*, to obtain the reputation of being Men of Virtue, and of an elegant taste. *Fourthly*, to acquire foreign airs, and adorn their dear persons with fine cloaths [*sic*] and new fashions, and their conversations with new phrases.[25]

In such a description as this, it is clear that the rewards of travel were to be gained only upon the return from it, in the form of affectations, memorabilia, and perhaps a bit of knowledge that would prove useful at home. Tucker generalized, of course; it is unlikely that all those mostly young men on the grand tours meant only to complete it. He also placed a certain responsibility on the travelers to know something of the places they visited: "For an ignorant traveler is of all beings the most contemptible: And the best that you can say of him is, that he sees strange sights in strange countries."[26]

In fact, one of the main intentions behind the grand tour during Queen Elizabeth's days was to cap a liberal arts education. But not all European society was amenable to the idea of young noblemen spending many months in idle travel. The philosopher John Locke was against it, and in conversations with a friend who supported such activity, is quoted to have ridiculed:

What a reasonable man wants to know is, the proper method of building up *men*; whereas your Lordship seems solicitous for little more than tricking out a set of fine *gentlemen*.[27]

But Locke thought travel was fine during one's maturity, and then it should extend well beyond Europe: "The tour of Europe is a paltry thing; a tame, uniform, unvaried prospect."[28] Locke thought one should instead travel to Asia or Africa, where true adventures could be found. If the gentlemen of his own time forwent Locke's advice, the modern adventure travelers have taken it to heart, for now the adventure travel industry directs itself mainly to developing new programs in Asia, Africa, and Latin America.

Modern adventure tourism distinguishes itself from the aristocratic travel of the grand tour less by intent than by technique. In both cases, the destinations are considered to be exotic, accessible only to those with an adventurous spirit and enough money. But places that were remote then are now commonplace, distance having been compressed by technology. Gentlemen on the grand tour traveled by foot, on horseback, or by traveling carriage; later aristocrats used more luxurious and speedy conveyances. Ocean travel aboard the colonial trading vessels marked the beginnings of a new and golden age of travel at the end of the nineteenth century. The names of such vessels, the *Rawalpindi*, the *Viceroy of India*, and the *Simla*, marked the colonial spheres of power to which the travelers were destined. The ships were equipped with private cabins, swimming pools, and gymnasiums, amenities enough to make one ship's captain remark:

We have been educated up to a standard of luxury that our forefathers never dreamt of. Even our second-class passengers want baths; they want a piano in their saloons; and they even want ice at their meals.[29]

Similar comments can be heard today throughout the adventure tour itineraries, where tour leaders guide visitors on pampered parades through the "lost worlds." A telling fact about such tours is that most aspire to places located in the Third World. This reminds us that the West's preoccupation with experiencing non-Western countries did not end with colonialism. Indeed, just as colonial tourism helped cement European ties to the colonies and produce the Western image of Third World places, so does modern tourism tie those same places to the new global economy. Whereas the former was invested in the material production of the Third World, so is the latter responsible for its continual reproduction. Moreover, both have included tourism in the mix of agents that have created the Third World—structurally, by a long history of dependency economics, and imaginatively, by the production of the Western concept of it. Accounts of the "Grand Days of Travel" aboard the colonial steamships and later along the world's railways fill the early pages of travel literature. The words intimate a romance with the wider world and a certain restlessness with the accustomed one. Greene, on an ocean trip to Africa, commented:

> But there are times of impatience, when one is less content to rest at the urban stage, when one is willing to suffer some discomfort for the chance of finding—there are a thousand names for it, King Soloman's Mines, the "heart of darkness" if one is romantically inclined.[30]

When travel became quick and easy, and the distances were diminished by new transportation, the grand tour became obsolete, an impossibility, and it was replaced by the organized tours that were being developed under the efforts of such entrepreneurs as Thomas Cooke. Travel became an industry and travelers properly became tourists, inclined to suffer less in exchange for a good adventure. The famed Orient Express, which made its inaugural run in 1883, Cunard's *Britannia*, whose 1840 maiden voyage marked the

beginning of cruiseline travel, and, later, airship travel all penetrated further into the unknown world for the new tourists who took trips like hunters bagging game.

It is ironic, if inevitable, that the contemporary adventure tours utilize even more sophisticated conveyances to transport clients into the places that are chosen precisely because they lack modernity. More so the fact that such tours spin a web of material security and comfort around the tour, and thereby isolate its members from the proximity of adventure, creating instead a diorama that meets the expectations of only the tourists. Such is the converse of travel, of course, where expectations are meant to be expunged, their premises dismantled by experiences.

Adventure travel has combined much of the elegance of the grand tour with contemporary themes of ecology and "rugged individualism" to fashion an incongruous tourism that is promoted as something daring and new, and other than itself. For example, the kind of appointments that are associated with cruiseline travel— stately staterooms, banquets, casinos, sunning decks—seem incongruous with the projected image of adventure travel, yet in 1992 Princess Tours introduced new "ecotours" to Alaska aboard its *Regal Princess*. The flagship will visit the Gulf of Alaska and its passengers will spend time on the remote Pribilof Islands, where they can view fur seals and explore bird rookeries in "rustic elegance." Alaska's flora and fauna, as well as its remarkable geology, have always held appeal for tourists, but without the new, highly suspect, label of "ecotourism." The current promotions capitalize on the fact that the market for adventure travel, while strong, remains a minor component of the tourism economy overall, and therefore it must be *developed* by the tourism industry— that is, designed, packaged, and marketed.

Ecotourism is an analog to adventure travel and a fashionable buzzword; it also constitutes a major new sales pitch. As awareness and concern about our natural world increase, the tours that convey a sense of environmental and social responsibility appeal to a growing niche of prospective tourists. Tourism experts agree that such a strategy works well. From airlines to travel agents to tourists, the message of adventure travel is that tourists can now travel with care and with a newfound sensitivity about the places they visit.

The travel sections of major newspapers and magazines are filled with glowing accounts of such adventure travel. Rather than telling how the tours show the places they visit, many of the articles show how such tours accomplish the tricky task of providing luxurious adventure. To sell the idea, the term "soft adventure modules" commonly is employed by the travel industry to describe what essentially are old-fashioned sight-seeing excursions to places that now happen to lie some distance off the well-beaten tourist track.

The number of agencies that package the adventure tours has swelled to many hundreds in North America alone. Among them, the oldest date to the Lindblad Tours and to Thomas Cooke, but most of the "groundbreaking" agencies are new—less than fifteen years old, and each year many additional firms are established. The newcomers to the industry often are decried by the older established adventure firms, who fear that more new tours inevitably will make the remote spots more accessible, encourage more development, and thereby undermine their appeal for the adventure travel market.

Indeed, adventure destinations can quickly become mass tourism destinations; the former, in fact, often act as harbingers of the latter. Examples of how adventure tourism has taken root in distant soils abound. Turkey, long portrayed as an adventure destination, now has a dynamic adventure tourism sector, tied to that country's sun, mountains, ocean, stunning history, and 142 official tourism centers. Bali, once a mysterious Hindu kingdom, is now a surfing mecca for Australian tourists and a shopping mecca for handicraft hunters.

The significance of adventure travel reverberates throughout the world where it occurs. It accounted for one-third of the small central African country of Rwanda's total annual revenue. At Wilderness Travel in Berkeley, California, adventure tour bookings have expanded by over 10 percent annually for the past decade and a half. In 1993 they offered 106 different packages on five continents. The geographical diffusion of adventure tours is astonishing, leaving few places and peoples untouched, covering literally Easter Island to Timbuktu. Patagonian cowboys now serve barbecues to tourists on the Argentine pampas, Balti porters carry trekkers' bags across the glaciers in the Hispar Valley of northern Pakistan's Karakoram mountain range, and seventy-three-year-old Chief Kini on the remote island of Ono in the Kadavu group of the Fiji Islands now shares bowls of ceremonial kava with tourists.

A 1991 article in the *Roanoke Times and World News* reports on adventure tours that lead to botanical camps in the Costa Rican highlands, to tree-planting expeditions to Nepal, to harp seal birthings on an ice pack in the Canadian Arctic, and to penguin counting in southern Patagonia. A writer for the *San Francisco Examiner*, in a 1988 article, described the experience of "Biking through Bali."

> The ride traversed a variety of landscapes: idyllic beaches, rich agricultural land, barren volcanoes, rain forests and lush canyons . . . our path wound along narrow country roads through lovely landscapes dotted with tiny villages where local traffic is light and tourist traffic is even lighter . . . The experience jarred my perceptions, heightened my awareness and invested the journey with a sense of absolute—and very desirable—removal from the set patterns of everyday life, and even a temporary dissolution of my usual sense of self.[31]

The various appeals of adventure travel—environmental conservation, commercial profit, national development, self-renewal, *dissolutions*, insure its steady if confused growth. Most of the travel section of the *New York Times* on May 19, 1991, was devoted to "Encounters with the Earth," an exposé of hard-hitting adventure travel that reads much like a commercial advertisement, hitting hard on imagery but soft on analysis.

One article describes how a French couple developed a lodge in the French Guinea rain forest first to service scientific researchers, but more recently to serve tourists. They now provide well-appointed bungalows, treks into the nearby jungle, and gourmet meals of peccary, tapir, and crocodile. The night sounds of howler monkeys and cicadas play background at the lodge to hit tunes from a generator-powered CD player. An article about such forms of tourism in the Brazilian Amazon quotes American ecologist Philip Fearnside:

> Green tourism is a good thing, but not something you can count on for protecting a lot of forest. Tourists find walking around a few acres to be enough. That doesn't provide economic justification for preserving hundreds of square miles of forest.[32]

Question: If green tourism does not provide an excellent rationale for keeping the forests green, then what kind of green does it provide? Answer: Banknotes.

Where it is a small fling, adventure tourism's role in national conservation development may well be minor, but the political and economic power of international tourism can be impressive when the numbers are large. A study by the Organization of American States predicts that by the late 1990s about 400,000 foreigners will participate in nature tours and other adventure travel packages in the Amazonian region alone. The governor of Amazonas state in Brazil, unlike his colleagues elsewhere in that country, has backed away in recent years from controversial pro-development stands for hydroelectric power generation, timber cutting, and farmland expansion in favor of the prospective tourist trends which demand intact forests. Recognizing the power of tourism, many of the conservation groups and educational institutions that ordinarily eschew commercial developments now join the commercial adventure travel agencies to offer opportunities for travel to the endangered environments that are located in the developing world.

The University Research Expeditions at the University of California, the Smithsonian Research Expeditions, the Foundation for Field Research, Earthwatch, and the International Research Expeditions are examples of scientific and education agencies that provide opportunities for tourists to join scientists on research trips to rain forests, archaeological sites, and village development programs. Other nonprofit, conservation-oriented organizations, such as the American Museum of Natural History, the Sierra Club, the National Audubon Society, the Nature Conservancy, and the World Wildlife Fund, also conduct adventure tours to remote places.

The tours offered by these groups may in fact be more informational than most of the commercial adventure tours, but they are compelled by a similar logic: that tourism may be both good ecology and good economy—it's a matter of emphasis. But the consequences of adventure travel, the ways by which it links world places and people, the manner of investment that it promotes in distant regions, the changes that it produces in environments and societies, and the images of world places that it shapes are all issues not yet made clear by its brief history.

4

Pushing into the Periphery

Thump, tump . . . Thump, tump . . . Thump, tump . . . An old woman using a foot pestle to pound barley delivered a dull wooden ring to the early morning. The melody sailed across the slate roofs of the village before it was muted in the hanging stillness of the valley and then lost to the silence of the mountain wind. Awakened from warm sleep, I jammed my hands into my pockets, squatted by the day-old fire, and blew shrouds of white frostbreath as I coaxed the coals to life. Chickens gathered about me, cackling and scurrying as hungry chickens do. A bell tinkled softly in the trees upslope, filling the air with a sound of icy crystals cut from the wintry silence. The ringing kept pace with the rustle of a lone, feeding cow. Pots rattled from inside one of the nearby shuttered homes. At the village spring, robed women were already filling weathered bronze vessels, *gagris*, with water for morning tea. Their soft murmurs of conversation drifted into the breaking day and mixed with the other early sounds until the hillside hummed in a predawn melody.

When the globe of the sun peaked over the eastern ridge, the village exploded in earthy colors: red chilies dry beneath golden cribs of shucked corn; the slate rooftops take on a dusky velvet glow as they leak smoke from the morning fires; stone pathways, polished from centuries of wear, catch the light and wind like ribbons of silver staircase among the tumble of rock and timber buildings. In the in-between light, women materialized from dark interiors and carried handlooms out to the centers of the courtyards. Beside them, their men carefully arranged sheaves of dry, split bamboo used to make *ghundries*, the local woven sitting mats. The day's activities thus began.

Below, and on both sides of the village, ledges of brown harvest rubble intermingle with flaxen terraces of ripe mustard in a six-thousand-foot cascade to the valley floor. The sonorous morning passage in the village is bounded by a sweep of ridges that fall away from the hamlet in three directions. Above the homes to the north, a thicket of oak and rhododendron trees extends upward to the hidden pastures. The damp forest muffles the upwell of village noise so that the white peak that spirals above the village remains undisturbed in its smug and deserved regality; the summit's stony silence sharpens the edge of the awakening village. The mountain is called Annapurna II, one of the giant peaks of the central Himalaya, and reaches a height of over six thousand meters above the village homes.

The drowsy tempo of the morning picked up after everyone drank the first cup of sweet milky tea: women began to weave coarse wool, their handlooms buzzing softly with the fiber; bamboo smacked against the courtyard stone as the strong male hands wove the chequered square *ghundries*; housemaids threw scraps of leftover food to the fowl with a mimicry of clucking noises. A loud rustle and a snort came from the buffalo stalls under the eaves of a nearby house as the animals were aroused and led off for the day in the fields. Young girls swept yesterday's dirt from the fieldstone terrace, raising clouds of dust that glistened and sparkled in the low sunrays.

Slowly, people left the family compound where I stayed. The first wife of the eldest son remained behind to continue her weaving and to prepare the midmorning meal—the first of the day. She was with child and excused from the heavy work in the fields. The grandfather also remained behind, to shape his *ghundri* and to nap a bit in the morning sun. The youngest son, a boy, took his charge of sheep and goats into the forest, en route to the upper pasture. I followed to keep him company and to see some of the high country above the village. We met the descending sunshine midway up the western slope and paused for a moment to enjoy its warmth. Continuing upward, the herder and his flock soon reached a rolling expanse of open grassland and shrubs. The white face of the mountain was at arm's length there in the crystal morning air; it seemed as if every icy crevasse and spiny rock ridge was discernible. Thin tendrils of the day's first cloud already wisped below the mountain face, following the contours of the lower slope. By noon, snow-bearing cumulous cloudforms would rise in the warming air, eventually to obscure the entire mountain.

Upon reaching the western side of the upper pasture, the boy hunkered down in the lee of a granite outcrop and squinted across the shortening shadows to the swale below. His animals drank at a frigid stream that appeared to drop from the liquid mists that clung to the far valley walls. That is where he left them when he journeyed back to the compound for the morning meal. His return through the forest was speedy, done in leaps and bounds. I kept up alongside him. We joined the others, already arrived, for rice and lentils washed down with watery yogurt. After everyone had eaten, the serving trays were collected by the small children and placed on the outdoor terrace for the family dog to finish. On a reed platform that jutted from the flagstone courtyard into the valley shadow, sat naked children. They alternated between lustful squeals of pleasure and pain as they bathed in buckets of steaming water heated at the hearth. Afterwards, they sat still with glistening bodies and matted hair as their mothers applied healing oils to moisturize their skin and hasten its darkening under the mountain sun.

When the morning rituals were complete, the family again quietly disjoined. The herder returned to his flock and the peace of the upper pastures. The youngest wife donned an ancient woolen shawl and hoisted a wicker basket to her back, fastening it across her forehead with a coarse tumpline. She used that to carry heavy loads of dungcakes and dry grass collected from the forest and pasture back to the compound, the dung to go into the compost, the grass for the livestock. She carried the basket with the strength of her neck muscles. The two eldest sons gathered together a few simple tools, a curved hand-scythe and a small spade, and descended to the mustard fields located at midslope. The harvest was almost at hand, and the work of pressing oil would soon begin at the water mills along the stream. The fields had been neglected for several days because of a village festival, and they needed to be weeded.

By late morning nearly everyone was gone from the courtyard for the day. The woman with child had departed for the stream to do morning laundry. Even the grandfather had slipped away, to while away some time in silent communication with lifelong cronies. Only the oldest woman and the youngest children remained behind; she was too old and crippled to walk much, they were too young for fieldwork. The two entertain each other throughout the day with the antics of the very old and the very young. During the brief winter afternoon the village is quiet. Occasionally a dog barked, transfixing the calm until someone hushed it with minced words or a thrown stone.

In the midafternoon, the valley winds arose, heading upslope, a prelude to the early dusk. The Buddhist prayer flags that towered over the village homes fluttered restlessly in the growing breeze, sending messages to heaven and casting fleeting shadows across the courtyards. The mountain, all but hidden now by a looming gray cloud, cast its shadow across the landscape. A shepherdess, crossing a distant ridge, was silhouetted momentarily against the mountain cloud backdrop, and then was obscured by the trailing dimness.

The sun slipped easily over the western ridge, prematurely it seemed, and the hillside relinquished the day. Villagers returned to their family hearths to prepare the evening meal, and lazily recounted the day's events around the warmth and the light of the fire. Outside, across the purple slopes, the sentinel mountain shimmered one last time through the darkening veil of clouds, flashed a wink in rosy conspiracy at the setting sun, and vanished. The black of the

Himalayan night quickly enveloped the village homes, and those who remained awake turned inward.

I was in the village of Siklis to observe the community, but I got caught, instead, in its rhythm. I was especially interested to see how it measured against the other Gurung villages that are located several days' walk away to the west, where mountain tourism is strong. The circum-Annapurna trekking circuit, one of the most popular adventure tourism sites in the world, was expanding, and Siklis, along with the other nearby Himalayan villages, would soon find itself well placed along the tourist trail. How such villages that retain much of their traditional ways will accommodate the new tourism economy interests the Nepalese government and development planners. But how the new commercial economy accommodates traditional life concerned me. The Gurung trace their lineage to Tibet, and have lived in central Nepal, among the slopes of the Annapurna massif, for over twenty-five centuries. They mix farming and herding, using the high pastures in the summer for grazing and the lower fields for planting grain crops. Their daily activities punctuate the longer seasonal rhythms that take villagers on a journey between the mountains and the valleys each year. Like many of the other Himalayan tribes, the Gurung people have followed their transhumance pattern for generations. It has allowed them to enjoy a great deal of autonomy, if not full isolation, in their lives.

The Himalayan tribes trade widely with the highlanders from Tibet and the lowlanders to the south, but for the rest of the world lying outside their mountains, they remain largely anonymous. The Sherpa tribes, living in the eastern part of Nepal, have become famous for the fact that they live in the shadow of the highest mountain on earth—Sagarmatha (Mount Everest), and share the spotlight of that summit with countless world-class mountaineering adventures.

The Gurung are famous worldwide for being the daring *Gurkha* soldiers, the "Gurkha Rifles," or "Johnny Gurk"—as they were known to the British soldiers—who were recruited by the British army to serve as mercenaries in their colonial battles. Stories are widespread about the exploits of those soldiers, their loyalty, amiability, and ferocity. It was said that a Gurkha soldier, if ordered in battle not to die, wouldn't. For a village boy to be chosen for the Gurkha regiment was a great honor, as well as a tremendous financial boon to his family. The military recruitment process was highly selective; only a handful of prospective soldiers was picked, but upon successful passing, a Gurkha recruit could expect to travel as widely as the British colonial empire was vast.

Gurkhas have served in such far-flung places as Burma, Belize, Hong Kong, and the Falkland Islands. Eventually, however, like most travelers, the warriors return home, to settle among the mountains of Nepal, where they inhabit one of the loveliest places on earth, a deep land cut by valleys and overtowered by such monstrous mountains as the Annapurnas, Lamjung, and Machupuchare—the sacred peak known for its shape as the "Fish Tail" Mountain.

When the first British Gurkha battalion was formed in 1815, the modern inroads to Gurung society were established.[1] There occurred an outmigration from the hill villages as generations of young men sought employment in the British and Indian armed forces. Returning soldiers brought back to their home villages a pension, material goods acquired abroad, and stories of the wider world. The mountain villages were connected to the colonial economy of Great Britain and that of the entire world via the recruitment of tribesmen who traveled, sometimes with their families, to distant outposts of the colonial British Raj, and who sent back service pay remittances to their families. In more recent times, many retired Gurkha soldiers, pensioned from the service, have returned to the villages of their birth and opened small lodges to accommodate some of the forty thousand Western tourists who come each year to these mountains.

Since the mid-1970s, when trekking became popular in the Himalaya, tourism in Nepal's Annapurna region has made considerable inroads into mountain society and has dramatically altered the mountain landscape. Signboards along the mountain trails announce the Gurkha-run lodges that are found now in many villages scattered across the region, from the valley town of Pokhara to the highland settlement of Ghandruk, which is now the regional center of a new, tourism-based conservation project. On the trekking routes, porters bearing tourist loads regularly pass mule traders hauling salt from faraway Tibet—old practices with a new twist. Village children eagerly greet tourists along the popular trails with rapid-fire cries of candy! rupee! pen! The ingress of tourism into the Annapurna highlands juxtaposes the new commercial economy with older subsistence ones, material affluence with poverty, and secular worldviews with those that see in the land all the possibilities of God.

Crossing Distances

The high peaks that physically bound the Gurung world delimit also the sacred inner realm of the high country; the Gurungs mark the trails into the mountains with religious shrines to honor the spirits that dwell therein. By thus signing the path, they mark also the journey into the mythic and supernatural worlds of the Gurung. The majestic mountains of Annapurna evoke awe but also humility; they render the Gurung universe complete, and the travelers who pass among them enter a moral order that ultimately is unfathomable, as elusive as the chimera of ice and snow on the mountain summits. Such a journey must be mediated by ritual and by ceremony. The Gurungs know this, as do native peoples worldwide, for whom the idea of culture and nature are practically inseparable, and they weave religious observances into the daily fabric of their lives. All over the world, we find, among the old ceremonies and cultural legends, similar markers of the spiritual journey. The ancient grotto paintings of Lascaux, the food taboos of the San Bushman of Africa, the totems of Native Americans living in the

Pacific Northwest region of North America, the Navajo sand paintings, Krishna dances in India, the Buddhist *thankas*, the Garden of Eden, all show the storied landscapes that define how one should properly live. And they all point to sacred elements of the physical world which unite people into cultures with supernatural origins.

Such things may be meaningless, however, to the thousands of newcomers who venture into these places as tourists from the modern, secular societies of the Western world. For them, reason rather than myth matters most. Logic, valuable as it may be in solving the puzzles of modern technology, proves less useful when dealing with the larger riddles of human consciousness. Across the world through time, the latter have required mainly spiritual approaches, and for guidance they demand knowing something of the old myths and stories. If contemporary Western society no longer holds a valid myth, as some assert, then that may be why people search other cultures—to discover that which may be lost in their own.

I often meet trekkers who go into the Himalaya regions purposefully to undertake the elements of a mythic journey, much as the overland travelers do in a more prolonged fashion. They attempt an abridged version of a mystic quest and see in their mountain trek the opportunity to quickly attain the main elements of a mythical journey: the *departure*, crossing the threshold into the imagined but still unknown places; the *initiation*, personal or spiritual annointments that require ritual and supernatural assistance; the *return*, the conquest of self, the completed quest, and the coming of the hero.[2]

In seeking out the high Himalaya, such travelers look for the *axis mundi*, the center point of the world which figuratively and symbolically may exist in the landscape—certainly for the Hindus and the Buddhists the mountains are that, especially Mount Kailash (but so is Harney Peak in South Dakota for the Sioux); ultimately, of course, it is found only within. As I remember my own companionship in such experiences, my recollections of the Annapurna trails are of making my way through blazing rhododendron forests, scrambling dangerously across frozen waterfalls, meeting a shaman in the woods whose presence was as ephemeral as the jasmine blossoms that flowered along the icy trail, and finding relief among the stone-and-timber huts of a village.

The many-layered half-memories of countless similar journeys take the shifting form of a fantasy, and I am reminded of the stories of British author J. R. R. Tolkien. His books, especially *The Hobbit* and *The Lord of the Rings* (a three-volume trilogy), masterfully catch the light and the shadow of a journey in Nepal; indeed, they are to be found among the most precious possessions of many stripped-down mountain trekkers, precisely because they weave tales as fanciful as the experiences tourists are likely to obtain in such a place as the Annapurna mountains.[3] So alike are the peaks, the forests, and the villages of Nepal to the fantastic landscapes of Tolkien, so common are the characters that resemble the cast of those stories— the Gandalfs and the Gollums and the "keepers of the inns by the side of the road"—that many travelers, without apparent validation, believe that Tolkien had once lived there, especially at a forested place called Ghorapani, when he conceived those remarkable stories. Like the shrines that the Gurungs place at the entries to their sacred mountain realm, passages from Tolkien's books (" . . . and the road goes forever on . . . ") inscribe the tourist landscapes, are found in the lodge ledgers, on restaurant walls, in numerous journals, such that they too become markers into a mystical landscape. The books simultaneously validate travelers' impulses and allow them to escape the often deplorable conditions at hand, when reality fails miserably to match the fantasy. The books are more than escapist literature, although that is how they may appear on the booksellers' shelves, but instead compose the structure and the motifs of a serious life journey.

When adventure tourists push at the perimeter of the world, they are doing more than connecting financial institutions or establishing other social linkages. They are entangling Western and non-Western concepts of life into an emerging image of a united world. This is the view we can gain from satellite glimpses of the earth, where political lines dissolve into great circulations of water, land, and air. A new mythology, one that connects distant places and peoples into a comprehensive and shared story of the past and the future, is implied by the participation of tourists on an adventure itinerary and rendered explicit in their creation by the adventure agencies. Consider:

> There is an undeniable fragility to our wonderful planet . . . cultures and ecosystems are increasingly threatened by our own actions and abuses. And with each passing day, tourism becomes more of a factor in the global condition . . . As the world turns "green," you'll find that at Wilderness Travel it's not a new color. We believe that adventure travel demands responsibility and sensitivity at both local and global levels. We also believe that the need to observe and experience "what lies beyond" is much more than a luxury for the privileged. Our adventures actively promote cultural preservation, conservation, and environmental protection. We have discovered that there is great power in experience. As you—world citizen and inquisitive traveler—experience the incredible human and natural wonders (and yes, the abuses) of our planet, you bring back a sharpened sense of place and a new perspective on your own culture and environment.[4]

and:

> The Art of Adventure Travel involves seeing beyond the new environment's surface, using all of your senses to connect with the essence of a place. It includes the native cuisine, but goes far beyond that. It means listening, with your inner ear, to the sounds of a place: the yak bells, the mother calling her child, the monk chanting, the wind whispering. It means feeling relaxed enough to let your tongue try out new sounds,

and then laughing just as hard as the locals at the results. It means watching the sun turn a snow-capped mountain from pink to gold in the stillness of early morning, and then imagining what role that daily occurrence plays in the peace of mind which pervades the local population. It means sitting in a tea shop, or wherever, and looking into the eyes and spirit of a fellow human being, and marveling at the similarity of people and the diversity of the human race. It means stretching your mind and imagination as well as your legs, and coming home a little richer than you left.[5]

When people say that the world is getting smaller, what they mean, of course, is that places are getting more connected. The geographers use the term *diffusion* to connote the spreading across space of innovations and ideas. Societies are forever coming up with new ways of achieving this—through technological advances in media and transportation, by advertising, and by electronic information exchanges such as computer mail—but people on the move still provide the most effective means of linking together distant world places and diverse cultures. Tourism outshines its rivals as the single most instrumental way of bridging distances precisely because it requires participation and experience. Both, however, frame the emerging viewpoints; hence, we end up with the diffusion of impressions rather than facts.

The adventure agencies, responsible for leading tourists into some of the most inaccessible locations on earth, play a responsible role in connecting such places to world events. The idea that this may not be a good thing is avoided in the adventure publications. Instead, adventure tourism is proffered in the light of acquiring a new worldview, a new way even of *measuring* life, a way of enabling people to find, in the distant places, their inner selves. That is the design of a myth. Although its initial conception may be commercial, it is enacted as all myths are enacted—departing from a known place for unknown trials and returning home anew. The places where such transformations may occur lie outside one's own common realm of experience. Geographically, this invokes the need for faraway places, new climates, unfamiliar cultures—places beyond the normal reach of one's life.

Since most such tourists come from the industrial urban centers of the West, the "beyond" quite naturally is found in the nonurban, pre-industrial frontier of the world economy that we know as the "Third World." But third implies a first and a second; while the latter remains dubious, the former quite clearly is the capitalist economies of North America, Europe, Japan, and a few scattered others. It is from the "first" world economies, the core regions of the modern industrial world where global wealth is accumulated, that adventure tourists come. Hence, by penetrating the world's perimeter as a means of acquiring "the beyond," adventure tourism links the peripheral economies of the Third World with the global economies of the Western world.

Yet, the "beyond" may not, in fact, measure up to the expectations of those on tour, having already given something of themselves over to modernity. Knowing this, the adventure agencies locate their itineraries at the very frontier of the Third World itself—places that are peripheral not only to the world economy but to their own respective national economies. Hence, a spatial divide occurs that signifies for adventure travel the destinations that lie in the farthest reaches of "beyond"—the *back of beyond*. But just as "Third World" suggests a first world, so does "back" suggest a front.

In a spatial sense, the back of beyond is the frontier of the world periphery—places furthest removed by physical access from global telecommunications, from personal and economic exchanges with "the outside"—places unto themselves. But in a touristic sense, the front is also that which is proffered to the tourists, where ceremonies are staged and lives are enacted for the sake of tourists' amusement. The "back," conversely, lies behind the scenes, where life simply is lived. That is where travelers seek to go, the place where consciousness is motivated, but it lies outside of tourism's normal grasp.[6]

At a national policy level, tourism regions may be opened and closed, tourist numbers may be limited, and the forms of contact between tourists and local people strictly regulated. The countries that favor tourism development in their frontier regions are still relatively few, despite the marked increase worldwide in the interest among tourists in adventure travel opportunities throughout the Third World. That is partly because, when measured against the revenue that is generated annually by mass tourism and mega-resorts, the income from adventure travel is small. For countries in desperate need of foreign earnings, it is less attractive than conventional forms of tourism. The restrictions on adventure travel also reflect the fact that the frontier territories of many Third World countries are only marginally controlled by the central governments. Boundary disputes, ethnic separatist struggles, and an overall lack of central planning characterize such places and make them inhospitable for many visitors and troublesome for most national governments.

There are many ways by which a country can regulate the incursions by tourists into the "back" of their national frontiers. For example, the Himalayan kingdom of Bhutan limits the numbers of Western visitors to only a few thousand each year who are allowed access to that country's spectacular mountainous landscape and Buddhist culture. The purpose of Bhutan's restrictive entry policy is to forestall the negative impacts that are seen to have accompanied the wave of tourists into neighboring Nepal.

The southeast Asian country of Burma allows visitors to enter that country for less than one week, and permits little spontaneous interaction between the tourists and the Burmese population. The Ecuadorian government, in accordance with the advice of scientists, is struggling with the number of visitors it should allow to visit the

Galápagos Islands; too small a number would mean economic hardship for the islanders who have come to depend on tourism, too many will quickly exceed the natural carrying capacity of the fragile island environment.

Such efforts to preserve the essential character of a country's "back" (as in *back*country, *back*ground, *back*water, or *back*ward) stem less from wanting to assure cultural integrity or environmental quality than from national insecurities over the control of the frontier regions. More common even than these policy issues are the distinctions made by local people between the contrived "front" where tourists are entertained and the unaltered "back." Sometimes, these divisions are matters of space. For example, tourists might be allowed access to parts of a village where the monuments and markets are located, but discouraged from visiting the residential parts where people live, work, and play. Nor would many tourists be inclined to go there, since it offers them nothing besides what it is—which may not be amusing in the least.

In other instances, entire pseudo-worlds may be created as "fronts" to shield the real worlds. A good example of this occurs in Fiji, where villagers at the Vatukirasa Village Ecotourism Culture Hotel Project have constructed an entire tourist village, complete with lodging and restaurants, in a design that exactly replicates the real village located next door. Tourists are restricted from visiting the village where villagers live, but are encouraged to stay at the pseudo-village, where they have the opportunity to experience local cuisine and ceremony and see local architecture and crafts-making without disturbing the actual habitat.[7] This arrangement came about as the result of efforts by an Australian entrepreneur who wanted to see a Fijian-owned and operated touristic venture. The resulting "model" village purportedly allows villagers to make money off their identity without losing it to the tourists.

Such a separation of self and image for commercial purposes seems improbable. The Fijian model invokes the very same ideas that we find in the theme parks of postmodern Western tourism, at least in design and conveyance, if not in actual place. But then, place may not overly matter when it is manufactured from the start. In Fiji, we are given the reproduction so that there is no need for the original.

It is curious to me that most efforts at tourism development in the frontier regions are initiated by persons who do not reside in them. The "back," apparently, is most readily distinguished by people not of it. Rarely have I found exceptions to that. For example, I know of no Gujar herder who designs the camel safaris in Rajasthan, although herders may wind up at some point leading them. I think that it would be unlikely to discover a hunter-gatherer conducting Amazonia rain forest river trips, or an Argentine cowboy running wilderness tours in Patagonia. Certainly, few, if any, monks would bother leading tours to disembodied monasteries in Tibet. And where insurgent groups threaten the central African countryside, I know of no guerrillas leading trekkers along the gorilla tracks.

An exception to the fact of outsider control are the Sherpas from Khumbu living in Kathmandu, who run trekking agencies in Thamel. Even there, with people frequently changing their names now to "Sherpa," it is difficult really to know who is from Khumbu. The fact that the adventure packages are designed and led by outsiders makes them similar to the other economic advances in the frontiers—the "beyond" always holds greatest appeal for those for whom it exists, surreally, as a place of unknown wealth.

The tourists who walk into the Himalaya enter a place of personalities as well as a place of mystery and spirit, a place that is inhabited by people who may be as wary as themselves. It is not a sneaking, unfounded suspicion, but rather an open one—a historical disinclination to fully welcome the advances of the outside world, in the form of foreigners, national bureaucrats, or people from across the adjoining ridge. The suspicions that many people who live in the margins harbor toward outsiders is historically driven, but it is balanced among some of them by a contemporary contentment with life, an acceptance that some call fatalism. It keeps some people at the periphery of the world, indisposed, but like a quiet eddy in a raging river, it offers solace. Ironically, the reluctance of some marginal people to conform to the advances of outer society turns out, in the end, to be alluring for the tourists who visit them. Perhaps it is a kind of kindred spirit, as Alastair Reid suggested:

> Gypsies, tinkers, travellers, vagrants—the more one looks into them, the more one discovers that civilization sets up its own discontents, and that the periphery is always inhabited either by those who are in flight from the center or by those who have been disinclined (perhaps from contentment, perhaps from suspicion) to move toward it. To be out, it seems to me, is not necessarily to be down, but at the same time it is difficult to see the inhabitants of the periphery as they are, without endowing them with self-conscious motives and turning them into champions of nonconformity. This they are not.[8]

More likely, however, the attraction of adventure tourists to indigenous cultures is one of opposites. People journey across immense distances to peer into the resolute eyes of others who live at opposite poles along the spectrum of life. To see them in some ways, inaccurately, as dissidents, rebels, shows a misplaced eagerness among tourists to know what life is like outside of their own conventions.

Distance matters little if that is the goal; those same people could probably find more true examples of such personalities living much closer to home. Nonetheless, it is common for travelers who spend long periods in the outlands to feel discontent with their own societies. This is nothing remarkable or anything new. It is, in fact, the genre of much of travel writing, found in the speculations of Henri Baudet, in the sexual fantasies of Flaubert, and in the anguished consciousness of D. H. Lawrence.[9] It invokes among seasoned travelers a certain wariness that allows them to meet head-on the personalities of their hosts.

For modern tourists, however, who seek pleasurable escape rather than refutation, the empathy of discontent is noticeably absent. This allows them to view, with a continued innocence, the stereotype of the "native." That fact underlies the success of the promotional materials of adventure travel, which continually produce false images, and it ensures the continual creation of new tours to new places. By placing its programs squarely into the world's frontier regions, the adventure tourism industry commercializes not only the geographical perimeter but also the periphery of the West's own disenchantment with itself.

Connections and Collisions

Most of the Annapurna trekkers follow a circuit that takes them north of the Nepalese town of Pokhara, on to the village of Ghandruk, and over a ten-thousand-foot pass to the Kali Gandaki River, where a string of villages stretches up the Thak Khola to the border regions of Tibet, or they walk farther up the Modi Khola, pass the village of Chumro and the summer grazing pastures, and into the fastness of the Annapurna Sanctuary. Those are the most frequented circuits in Annapurna since the region opened to foreigners and became a popular trekking region in the late 1970s. But now, since alternative trails have been established in the eastern part of the Annapurna Conservation Area, the more remote villages such as Siklis have joined the mountain trekking world. Every year, as the new routes are devised to open new territory to the tourists, the geography of tourism extends to places that are rooted in much older traditions.

As it pushes into the heart of the Gurung world, adventure travel inexorably stretches its reach, not only to the world's frontiers, but to the very edges of human consciousness. As they enter religious ground—places that have been made sacred by the practice of the people who live there—the tourist trails leading into the high Himalaya span the secular worlds of the visitors and the sacred world of the native mountain people. While the bond between land and spirit may be severed in modern Western society, the traditional cultures of the world maintain their vital link to the earth. The abyss that travelers peer into as they approach the otherworld is that which separates their own world of logic and reason from one of mystical intuition. In spanning this divide, adventure travel may cover its most important distance.

The geographer Stan Stevens found that the Gurung tribes, while assisting in tourism development by running the lodges and serving the tourists who visit their home region, also have a unique way of mediating the annual invasion by tourists of their spiritual, inner mountain world:

> Lodgekeepers from the sanctuary and the upper gorge devised a new ceremony. Gathering at the shrine in the gorge as they head home after closing their lodges for the monsoon, they offer prayers to the Barahar, as a way of atoning for offenses their guests might have caused in crossing the threshold between the ordinary universe and a sacred realm.[10]

The Latin origins for the concept of a sacred dwelling place is *cultus*, from which comes our word *culture*. This etymology implies not just a location, as the word *place* ordinarily suggests, but a more comprehensive notion of relations that are mediated through ceremony, a religious geography that requires participation. Adventure tourism carries Westerners literally across that chasm between *space* as the institutional, geometric, non-absorbed phenomenon and *place* as the sacred hearth—space with meaning that is derived from experience and belief. But it may not prepare them with the knowledge that such distinctions lie within them.

Adventure tourism remains grounded in the predilections of Western society. Important among those is the concept of private land ownership. It is embedded in the Western psyche and collides with the alternative notion of many native geographies that land is sacred and held in common. The implications of such a collision are considerable because, as the poet and essayist Gary Snyder has pointed out:

> If even some small bits of land are considered sacred, then they are forever not for sale and *not for taxing*. This is a deep threat to the assumptions of an endlessly expansive materialist economy.[11]

Tourism is foremost an economic activity and subscribes to the essential formulations of classical economic thought. It brings to common lands in the periphery the market forces that so completely govern Western society, causing a divide in the way traditional people view their land; economic valuations transfigure other ways of seeing the landscape and fragment them, creating a pastiche that changes rapidly with shifts in perspective and economic conditions.

The purpose of the Gurungs placing shrines along their trails into the mountains is not to show the literal path—that is easily distinguished and learned at a young age—but to mark the metaphysical way into a land that is *in its entirety a shrine*. The guideposts into that realm, unlike the rock cairns placed strategically to show hikers crooks in the path, are incapable of being exact, precisely because they point into the wilderness—the organic world of land, culture, and the supernatural.

It is across that chasm that the classical travelers and many of the overlanders leap, sometimes with success, but which most modern adventure tourists never quite attempt. Perhaps that is because

Western society, at least the Euro-American society from which most tourists come, has not had sufficient time living in one place to understand the deep connections that other cultures have established with their land. Maybe that is possible only after many centuries of staying put. When people live in a place, they shape it to their desires, but if they stay long enough, it is they who will be most changed.

The historically charged view of Western society toward the land is multifarious; it tends to view the landscape in several ways: as historical artifact—an indelible record of human settlement and achievement; as aesthetic—"pretty as a picture postcard"; as a means of acquiring wealth through development or use; or, most recently, as a disturbing or blighted scene.[12] These "views" of the landscape derive from the mind, but they are anchored in human experience that has a material base; thus they reflect the political, social, and environmental milieus that shape our thoughts and ourselves. They are, after all, *regulated* views.

I think that such views stem also from a temporary occupancy of a place, and hence they contrast with those of native people who have lived in the same spot for centuries, who rarely see the land in objectified or even romantic terms; rather, for them, the land is sustenance and inseparable from their condition of life—not something to be looked at so much as felt. And so when tourism pushes at the world periphery, it moves across a space that links both forward to new interpretations of the world and backward to old appraisals and lifeways.

After all, geography is to space what history is to time; they both provide a context for our experiences. Maybe it is optimistic to think that such connections can still be understood by Western society and practiced by its citizens. By their responsible entry into the private worlds of old traditions, sensible tourists might discover yet the means to do so. Perhaps that is what Snyder had in mind when he wrote:

The temples of our hemisphere will be some of the planet's remaining wilderness areas. When we enter them on foot we can sense that the *kami* or (Maidu) *kukini* are still in force here . . . The best purpose of such studies and hikes is to be able to come back to the lowlands and see all the land about us, agricultural, suburban, urban, as part of the same territory— never totally ruined, never completely unnatural. It can be restored, and humans could live in considerable numbers on much of it.[13]

Even in the modern world of consumption, where the remote places are visited mainly for their scenic value, tourists may share in the reconstruction of places. Indeed, the tourism landscape itself, a product of capitalism and leisure, when extended to the non-Western world, reinvents places for touristic consumption and offers all kind of possibilities for meaning. But what it fails to comprehend oftentimes is that the historical development of places may, in fact, have nothing to do with tourism. Regional identities are shaped by natural and cultural histories, forces of politics and society; where these converge to form an attractive setting, tourism may add to the more recent history of the regional landscapes. But most likely, it subtracts much of the complex history of a place, simplifying and decontextualizing it for the easy consumption of tourists.

The southern part of Mexico, where the Sierra Madre Occidental and the Sierra Madre Oriental converge in a jumble of rugged mountains, contains the Valley of Oaxaca. It is easy to understand the appeal that Oaxaca has for tourists. The city occupies a lovely physical setting, the town nicely mixes colonial and modern influences, and the nearby Indian villages offer diverse excursions for archaeological sightseeing and for visiting the weekly markets. More appealing even than the material aspects of the region are the ethereal images provoked by Oaxaca's mountain landscape, its old

cultural patterns, and its exquisite architectures. According to one travel writer:

> Do you know of these fairy tales in which a wandering bu-
> colic slips down a hole in the ground or the back of a cavern
> and finds himself in another world altogether, a world of
> good, kind, and shining? That's rather how I felt when, on
> my first afternoon in the Mexican town of Oaxaca, I walked
> down to the *zocalo* . . . [14]

The elusive qualities of Oaxaca that now endear it to tourists have a history that greatly precedes them. It is a complicated history of indigenous people overtaken by colonial missions, of blending influences, and of transformations by the efforts of the modern Mexican state. The Mixtec and Zapotec people, whose cultures flourished in Oaxaca for a millennium before the Spanish conquest of Mexico in the sixteenth century, were responsible for construct-ing the extraordinary city-states that controlled the valley. They also cleared and farmed the countryside, lived in self-contained villages, established regular weekly markets throughout the coun-tryside, and fought wars among themselves and against invaders.

The Spanish colonialists brought to Oaxaca a new language and a new religion. They built magnificent Catholic churches, planned the towns along a European grid design, and introduced a new language, food, and music. The colonial innovations eliminated or augmented the Indian cultural influences to arrange a wholly new cultural landscape in Oaxaca.

The Indians reside still in the valley, giving Oaxaca one of Mexico's strongest Indian influences. But their culture, largely displaced by the region's colonial history and by modern national-ism, hangs on only slimly in the villages. It surfaces today all too often in the guise of tourist excursions to the handicraft villages. Such places as Teotitlan de Valle (a Zapotec weaving village) and San Bartelo de Cayotepec (famous for its black pottery) have turned

over almost exclusively to tourism. Galleries and studios in those
villages open to visitors and almost every household is involved in
producing handicrafts.

The cultural history of Oaxaca marks the landscape most indelibly with the region's famous pre-Hispanic ruins. Monte Albán and
Mitla, two of the most important archaeological sites in all of
Mesoamerica, bring tens of thousands of tourists to Oaxaca every
year. The villages, the ruins, and the weekly markets held in the
Indian towns, are common excursions now for tourists from
throughout the world. Lynn Stephen, an anthropologist who has
worked among the Zapotec people in the village of Teotitlan de
Valle, sees in the promotion of Oaxaca tourism the commercialization of Indian life:

> To capture the interests of tourists, particular features of cul-
> tural and material production were commoditized and
> packaged for sale by the federal government. The ideological
> package that was and is sold to tourists who came to states
> with high indigenous populations is based on a homogenized
> image of "Indian culture" and the material remains of that
> culture that can be visited or purchased and taken home.
> Of primary import in this cultural package is the Mexican
> Indian.[15]

The construction of Oaxaca's tourism landscape has contributed
important wealth to the local economy. Many new buildings and
infrastructure improvements describe much of the valley and attest
to the newfound wealth. But Oaxaca manages also to retain a vitality
and elegance that is rare in those places where we find tourism to be
a strong component of the local economy. The attention of tourists
to the history and material culture of Oaxaca is legitimized by the
designation of the valley as a UNESCO world heritage site.

Oaxaca simultaneously remains a popular spot on the overland
travel circuit and a conventional tourism destination. The curious

success of Oaxaca as both a travel and a tourist destination may be limited, however, to its current transitional history. Certainly, Mexico has grand plans for the further development of tourism in that state, particularly along the coastal regions near the fishing village of Puerto Escondido. The valley of Oaxaca, its mountain landscape, Indian villages, ruins, farmland, and the central city of Oaxaca shape a distinctive region within southern Mexico.

I can imagine how, under the auspices of the UNESCO world heritage claim, it may retain its unique appeal for tourists. But I find it less conceivable to imagine how it will continue to accommodate the local interests of the Indian people. For today, as the villages become part of the travel agency itineraries, the connections between places in Oaxaca become less historical and more commercial—part of an evolving "Oaxaca Grand Tour." At the main hotels in Oaxaca, one now finds travel agents offering group tours by bus to the ruins and to the handicraft villages. The tendency exists to "fossilize" history for touristic preservation, but to disallow the continuity of those heritages which give places such as Oaxaca their important vitality.[16] As it moves through the transition from its position on the overland traveler's "Gringo Trail" to its newfound prominence as an international tourism destination, the authority of Oaxaca's local cultural character will confront the force of tourism.

The power of consumer tourism is suggested by the geographer Robert Sack, in his explorations of the consumer's world, as he shows how it ties to the construction of places and the designation of spatial relations, as well as the identity of oneself:

> Creating tourist places embeds the tensions of commodities into the landscape. Tourist attractions can become like other places by providing familiar accommodations and foods. They can become distinct by supporting or reinventing local customs. They can make us part of a group by catering to a

certain clientele. They can help us find ourselves by offering us self-absorption or by assisting our escape to an exotic place; through the process of immersing ourself in a place, we come to discover our true identities.[17]

As purveyor of a material economy, tourism extends its influence not only to the way land is imagined, but also to the way it is managed. This is most curious because, until recently, indigenous systems of land management have worked quite well. Throughout the non-Western world, we find the places and the cultures where tradition and spirit, maintained across the passage of time and sometimes vast distances, define environmental outlooks.

In Australia, for example, aboriginal culture stayed alive by knowing its land through its music. Songlines—rhythmic memories of such topographical features as prominent ridges, cliffs, and hidden valleys, important dry season waterholes and springs, initiation sites and other ceremonial places—define the vast territory of the aborigine's epochal *Dreamtime*, the beginning of time, and they show the way into the spiritual landscapes of the past by following along the tracks of the old people. These pathways are now crossed in places by new tourist trails, where the Dreamtime traditions and the rambling, nomadic travel known to aborigines as the *walkabout* have developed into new adventure travel itineraries. Led by some tribal elders and newly appointed guides, the tourist excursions into aboriginal landscapes nonetheless barely scratch the veneer of the deeply sacred places.

In the Pacific, among the Hawaiians, the ancient gods are manifest in nature—from Maui, the demi-god who pulled the Hawaiian archipelago from the seabed into creation, to Pele, the wild-haired fire goddess who is embodied in the destructive power of the volcanic eruptions. The locations where such deities are worshipped contain *heiaus*, temple sites that have a strong spiritual power known as *mana*. The *heiaus* bound traditional Hawaiians together in a religious system that emphasized the fecundity of the land and its sacredness. They also legitimized the power structure that ruled the islanders' lives under the control of the *ali'i* royalty and thereby connected the organization of culture with the organization of the land. The *heiaus* differ by their function, such that we find in the Hawaiian landscape *heiaus* devoted to fishing, to farming, to navigation, or to war and human sacrifice.

Many of the deities of ancient Hawaii and the rest of Polynesia link not only to the land, but to the sea, from which the earlier mariners came and to which all souls eventually depart. Today in Hawaii, one commonly finds leaves of the sacred *ti* plant and other offerings placed at the altars of the *heiaus,* indicating that the old religions are still practiced. But more commonly seen are the tour buses that daily unload hundreds of passengers at the popular temples, who scamper amidst the ruins, and for whom such places provide mainly photo opportunities.

In the wet forests of equatorial Cameroon, located in western Africa, the Baka hunter-gatherers sing songs to the forest, mimicking the animals they hunt, recounting important historical events, and telling myths. For the Baka, the deep jungle is filled with spirits and to venture there, which the Baka do on a daily basis, is to confront the soul of the forest and the spirit of life itself. Further east, in the central African countries of Rwanda and Burundi live the Mbuti forest dwellers. Like the Baka, they live a semi-nomadic life, hunting animals, foraging, and practicing minor horticulture in a habitat that historically has been undisturbed. But times have changed for the forest dwellers.

The deep rain forests of central Africa were first penetrated by Western adventurers when Dr. David Livingstone visited the region in the 1850s. Now, in the 1990s, several dozen adventure itineraries take thousands of tourists annually into those same forests, offering new opportunities to learn old bushcraft—"penetrating the bush," hearing the "calls of the wild," and following tracks, scat, and "rubbing places."[18] The adventure tours focus especially on the vicinity of Zaire's volcanic landscapes at Virunga National Park and, until recently, on Kigali in Rwanda, where tourists could join the "Ultimate Primate Safari" or the "Gorilla Tracking Trip" to see the mountain gorillas made famous by the research of Dian Fossey and the cinematography of *Gorillas in the Mist.*

In Nepal, the mountains are named for the deities that dwell therein and which regularly intervene in the lives of ordinary human beings. The tourists who visit those places may know such things—indeed, the adventure agencies market them as part of the tour—but they cannot by reason or by abstraction appropriate them as their own. Such beliefs remain the possession of the inhabitory people, but often become the amusement of the tourists. The ritual that governs tribal life, especially that that is steeped in local environmental lore and that mediates how villagers conceptually and practically organize their worlds, becomes part of the tourist package.

With the increasing attention paid to atmospheric and land degradation worldwide, environmental concerns are now shared everywhere; along adventure tourism's path, where the scientific efforts of the Western world meet the supernatural rituals of the native cosmologies, the West's regulated ways of observing the landscape meet the no-view-at-all of the indigenous people. Everywhere in the world, where tourists enter the sacred realms, they hit a wall. Beyond lies something incomprehensible—at least, without the proper training. Those same tourists, however, may be well trained in the clinical knowledge of their own societies and have an interest in such issues as cultural and biological diversity.

Many of the adventure tours call attention to serious environmental plights that degrade the landscapes around the world, including those which the tours will visit. The tourists are not isolated from such realities; indeed, they are promoted as part of the package and, especially for the ecotours, may become the raison d'être for the trip. Under the best of circumstances, as the traditional places change with the advent of tourism, the secular understandings of Western science and tradition combine with the environmental and spiritual knowledge of the native peoples. That, at least, is the hope of the advocates of adventure tourism who argue that it will promote among visitors a heightened sensibility about the natural world.

In Nepal, where the privatized interests of the tourism economy reach the common lands of the indigenous mountain tribes, the inroads made by environmental institutions—mainly, national parks and protected areas—often become paramount. Today, such environmental interests frequently converge with those of tourism.

Such is the case in north central Nepal, where the Annapurna Conservation Area Project (ACAP), established in 1986 under the auspices of the King Mahendra Trust for Nature Conservation, provides a comprehensive environmental management program for the mountains of the Annapurna region. It serves also to promote touristic development in the region, albeit with the caveat that it should be done with conservation and heritage goals in mind. ACAP holds a viewpoint that arises from an unorthodox blend of science and native knowledge. In that way, it may be an innovative attempt to sustainably develop a landscape for the tripartite goal of meeting local needs, tourism, and national development. The message of ACAP to local residents and tourists alike is to use the land sustainably, to see its fragility under the mighty visual weight of the mountains, and to accept often novel ways of observing and managing the land.

In effect, ACAP relies on local knowledge initially to inform its programs, but finally it asks the hill tribes to accept exotic regulatory practices and to embrace a viewpoint that shows borrowed scenes—national parks, environmental conservation areas, protected refuges. No matter how necessary these views may be, or how well-intentioned the overall program is, the fact that it asks people to change not only their behavior but also their worldview means that the long-term success of such programs as ACAP remains unclear.

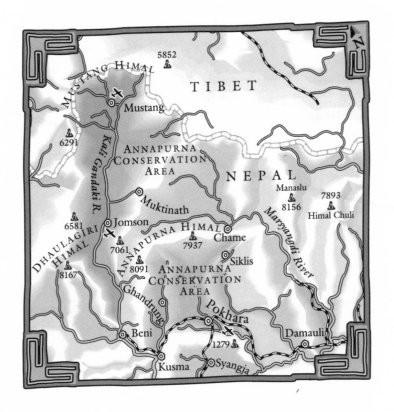

Dr. Chandra Gurung, a former classmate of mine and currently the director of ACAP, is keen to see that controlled tourism remains a central feature of that region's environmental development. But tourism management often means tourism growth, and in the case of Annapurna, such growth is spidering into watersheds and ridges that hitherto remained out of tourist bounds. Dr. Gurung's home village of Siklis lies along one of tourism's spreading tentacles. Many residents of that village see in this expansion a great potential for new economic opportunities in their community. They see that with the coming of electricity and roads, lodges and wealth, a material prosperity may occur that has never before existed in their village. But less visible to them are the long-term costs that their community will bear as the tourism economy penetrates their intimate world. A loss, if you will, of rhythm.

Quixotic Searches

One of the confounding facts about tourism is that it cannot stay still—it has, at least, that much in common with travel. Adventure tourism, especially, constantly seeks out new places and new experiences for its clients, who are in search of the elusive "authentic." This quest continually propels people further into the remote places, as the former destinations, changed and made accessible, lie awash in tourism's wake. One of the main facts about adventure travel is that, in its search for "authenticity" in the undisturbed places, it continually pushes the tourism frontier farther into the world's periphery, contributing to the continued geographic expansion not only of national and global economies, but of the commercialization of places. Money, however, rarely buys the truth, and in exchange for the admittance fee, cultural tourism sites most often simply put on a show. Unlike the cultural tours, natural history tours—the so-called ecotourism—do offer possibilities for authentic experiences, at least initially, while the habitats remain pristine. But as nature tourism progresses, these places, too, will inevitably be affected by visitors' demands for services and conveniences.

The adventure tours confront the disturbing fact that, in their search for authenticity, the tourists dispel the very qualities which they seek. In Nepal, for example, jaded trekkers commonly avoid the favorite trekking circuits because they feel that the villages en route have, themselves, become jaded toward the tourists. In the South Pacific, where hula dancing, fire-walking, and ceremonial feasts are now staged shows, tourists seek the bluer lagoons of the "outer islands." The tropical idyll, it seems, is being pushed ever further out to sea. Dearden describes it this way:

> As The Real Thing comes into increasing contact with tourists, it becomes a little less of The Real Thing as the mixing of cultures, values, and economy serves inevitably to dilute the strength of the original culture. Tourists are no longer satisfied with this dilute strength culture, partly of their own making, and hence go to see The Real Thing elsewhere, which soon suffers the same fate.[19]

The search for authenticity ultimately consumes itself. It promotes an external orientation among those very cultures and environments that tourists initially seek out precisely because they remain inward looking. This is an ultimate irony of adventure travel; like the quixotic search for the holy grail, adventure tourism's quest for validation is self-defeating.

In a recent article that appeared in the *Annals of Tourism Research*, Ira Silver wrote that Westerners look for "authenticity in the non-Western Other because modern life has undermined the connections between them."[20] The "other" he is writing about is the non-Western, idealized "primitive" people of the world, people whose touristic identity is given to them, not by their own cultural histories, but by the imaginations of Westerners. The connections he refers to are not made explicit, but presumably they are between society and nature.

In giving native cultures an alter-identity, the tourists do not succeed in taking away the cultures' real identities, and if in seeking out the "primitive," tourists look for ways to be wild, it is only for a short time. Even then, they tend not to see, hidden behind the ceremonies and the masks, the poverty and the suffering that would dismay them. The modern urban life from which most tourists come is, after all, nothing if it is not the antithesis of wildness, for which "primitive" is taken not as a condition of life, but as a dignified way of relating to the world. If adventure quests are a reflection of that, then they should not be seen as peculiar to themselves. Gary Snyder relates the amusing and insightful story of a young woman anthropologist who visited a community of the Haida tribe in North America. The anthropologist asked a Haida elder woman, "What can I do for self-respect?" The elder replied, "Dress up and stay home."[21]

What tourists believe to be "authentic" has everything to do with what they see to be real. The problem is that much of the Western consumer's world is fundamentally unreal—produced, packaged, and promoted exclusively for consumption. Consequently, as premier consumers, the tourists confront the disturbing fact that most of what they imagine will be something other than what it is.

Umberto Eco, in his book *Travels in Hyperreality*, distinguished between that which is historically authentic and that which is visually inauthentic. According to Eco, we are trapped in the pseudo world of fabricated imagery:

> Everything looks real, and therefore it is real; in any case the fact that it seems real is real, and the thing is real even if, like Alice in Wonderland, it never existed.[22]

Such a world of hyperreality is filled with levels of illusion, much like the Hindu's world of *maya*, and the role of humankind is to expose the illusions. This rarely occurs, however, since it usually is more convenient to maintain the front of illusion and it may, in fact, be impossible to discard it.

Most tourists choose to keep the false image of places they visit, which is in part their own making, so that they should not feel so out of place. Almost exclusively, tourism initially constructs the visual imagery of a place and then consumes it as "scenery." Visual "authenticity," like the other forms of it, may be impossible to achieve, since the "view" largely is in the mind of the viewer. As sightseers, tourists select the scenes that they enjoy and photograph. This act may distance tourists from a place, allow little empathetic connection between them, and relegate to visitors a certain peripheral position in the overall experience.[23] A common product, therefore, of "sightseeing" is the photograph—a two-dimensional result of a rather flat experience. Moreover, as a visual record of a place, most photographs also lack authenticity. They invariably show edited, "cropped" versions of a landscape, where the unsightly or uninteresting scenes are removed from the line of sight by aiming the camera lens. The editing of travel snapshots is a metaphor of the overall edited tourism product, but registers an image that lingers in the memory.

The photograph, perhaps more than any other single achievement of tourism, signifies the importance of obtaining a record of places that are visited:

Even more than travel, tourism relies on the visual—the scene, the view. Photos and postcards are the tourist's means of capturing a trip and experiencing it again and again.[24]

For some tourists, the photographs may become more than a record of the journey, a sort of documentation; they become the journey.

Most important, they define what is seen and, therefore, what is consumed by the tourists in the places they visit.

A curious fact that often distinguishes travelers from tourists is that the former rarely carry cameras, while the latter always do. According to John Steinbeck, "One goes not so much to see but to tell afterwards." Photographs are excellent proof of the journey. For many tourists, a place may not be worth visiting at all if it cannot be photographed. One year, I joined a European companion on a month-long hike to Mount Everest Base Camp in the Khumbu region of Nepal. Five days into the trek, my friend ruined his camera while crossing a swollen river. It seemed incredible to me at the time, but rather than continuing into the mountains without it, "sightless" as it were, he chose to abandon the journey and return to Kathmandu.

One of the common missions of diverse adventure tourism programs is to provide opportunities for taking photographs. The visual record seems to be paramount among the adventure itineraries. But photographs are not simply documents, they are *ways of seeing* the world. Where fine art photography offers all the possibilities for creative vision, snapshot photography may instead conceal the world that lies beyond the camera's lens, reducing the elusive quest for the picturesque to a mere mechanical means of capturing it, and thereby dissolving travel experiences to souvenirs. Photographs fit well with the needs of tourism, especially adventure tourism, partly because, as Susan Sontag has explained, both are fundamentally consumptive yet never are really satisfied:

> The final reason for the need to photograph everything lies in the very logic of consumption itself. To consume means to burn, to use up—and, therefore, to need to be replenished. As we make images and consume them, we need still more images, and still more. But images are not a treasure for which the world must be ransacked; they are precisely what is at hand wherever the eye falls. The possession of a camera can

inspire something akin to lust. And like all credible forms of lust, it cannot be satisfied: first, because the possibilities of photography are infinite; and, second, because the project is finally self-devouring.[25]

That tourists may be photographing simple illusions appears not to matter at all. Coming from a world of pseudo-places, where the boundaries of realism constantly blur with those of made-over places, it is questionable whether Western tourists actually bother to seek the authentic at all. Most tourists, particularly those who seek adventures among other cultures, would find unintelligible or simply uninteresting the true displays of foreign life; they would rather get what they already expect. The adventure tourists who quite literally drop into exotic settings from outer space have not sufficient time to adequately immerse themselves in local realities, to become oriented to a new place.

Much like a passenger disembarking from a high-speed train at an unknown station, tourists need time simply to get their bearings. That is impossible in most of the short trips offered by the adventure itineraries. The adventure tour agencies know this, which is why they provide tours to match, or even exceed, the tourists' expectations and which, in the end, leave little need for true adventure:

"Better than I ever imagined—and I imagined a pretty good trip."
"I saw more gorillas, apes, and monkeys that I ever dreamed."
"The Great Pyrenees Traverse surpassed all my expectations."[26]

Preferences for the pseudo adventures over the true adventures turns the very word "adventure" into a cliché. While the goal of adventure travel purportedly is to provide unique and compelling experiences from which tourists may learn more about themselves and the places that they visit, it succeeds best at turning the truly extraordinary into something ordinary and the places into souvenirs. According to Daniel Boorstin:

> ... while an "adventure" was originally "that which happens without design; chance, hap, luck," now in common usage it is primarily a contrived experience that somebody is trying to sell us.[27]

In marketing the image of "adventure" among the peripheral places on earth, adventure travel succeeds also in imparting an image of the Third World. For most of its clients, who have little contact with non-Western places outside of their experiences with the adventure catalogs and the tours themselves, this image overshadows any that they might otherwise obtain from a closer reading of those same locations. While it may be argued that the "Third World" has always been a construction of the West—the work of colonialists, politicos, and social scientists, and more recently immigrants, now we have untold opportunities to experience for ourselves its outlandish character as a travel destination. This goes beyond the resort developments that have been situated for quite some time in Third World countries—mainly because they occupy the tropics. Nowadays, it is the frontier regions of distant Third World countries that preoccupy the imaginations of prospective adventure tourists.

The Creation of Adventure Places

Tourists love to tinker—with their tent poles, cameras, airline tickets, and then with lodges, roads, and amusements, until they transform the very nature of places. That is tourism development. Adventure tourism, like the other forms of economic growth, enlists an impressive assembly of mechanical allies to assist in its development. Although it seeks places that lie off the beaten track, such tours rely heavily on roads to get them into proximity.

To facilitate tourist travel to the remote national parks and to other adventure tourist regions, the governments of many Third World countries have embarked on a road-building frenzy. For example, in 1965, when Nepal opened to mountain tourism—it was in 1964 that Colonel Jimmy Roberts offered his first mountain itinerary and three persons signed on—the country had a total of only 289 kilometers of paved road. In 1983, when tourism was well established, it contained 2,322 kilometers. That may not be much when compared to the car culture of North America, but by Himalayan standards it shows the region's steady investment in roadbuilding projects that help to subdue the intractable mountain landscape. Much of the new road construction in Nepal is located in the Tarai valleys, and is meant to tie together western and eastern sections of the country. But several additional north-south feeder roads have been built also in the mountain regions to assist in more widespread regional development programs.[28]

The roads do more than carry tourists, they forge national identities in the frontier territories, bring to remote people the dubious benefits of development, and connect the distant places. But just about everywhere that we find roads in Nepal, we also find groups of Westerners on an adventure. The mountainsides in Nepal frequently reverberate with dynamite charges as the new roads are carved into the land; the blasts rip across the landscape carrying the winds of change. As the hillsides are carved by the new roadway terraces, the tourism trails overlay the old travel circuits. Buses now ply the road from Kathmandu to Jiri, a village located along the walking trail to the Khumbu region of Sagarmatha (Mount Everest), cutting the travel time to the Sherpa homeland by one-half; the roadhead north of the trading town of Dhumre in west-central Nepal shifts farther up the Marsyangdi River each trekking season, making the upper reaches of the valley more accessible to more tourists; Langtang National Park, located north of Kathmandu, can now be reached by truck along the hazardous road situated above the Trisuli River en route to the village of Dhunche.

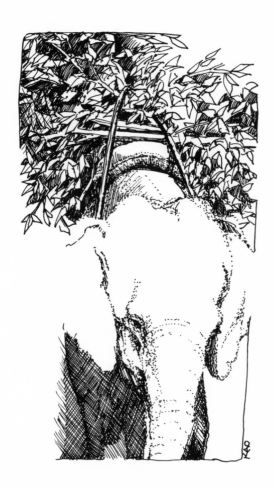

Those roadways, and others like them throughout Nepal, bring less intrepid tourists to the brink of adventure destinations; they also push the most remote and therefore desirable ("authentic") places further away for the seasoned adventure tourists. Thus by enhancing accessibility to adventure tour regions, they also ensure the creation of new ones. In fact, adventure destinations are constantly formed, both physically by new roads, lodges, parks, and other institutional developments and conceptually through the promotional developments of the adventure tourism industry. In its 1993 catalog, Wilderness Travel listed 106 different trips, 35 of which were new for that year. The new itineraries included "Zimbabwe Adventure," "Arabia Felix: A Journey through Yemen," "Osiris: Land of the Pharaohs," "Realm of the Medici," "The Hidden Monasteries Trek" in Tibet; "Snow Lake Glacier Trek" in Pakistan; "Voyage to Vietnam," "Castles, Samurais, and Legends" in Japan, "Serious Fun!" in New Zealand, and many others with equally enticing titles.

Two pages of the 1993 catalog were devoted to "Nepal's Forbidden Treks," an outline of new tours to the regions of Mustang, Manaslu, Dhaulagiri, Dolpo, and a trans-Himalayan trek across most of Nepal's border region. Here is what it says about these new prospects:

> After years of rumour, Nepal's once forbidden trekking regions—Mustang, the Dhaulagiri Himal, Dolpo including Shey Gompa and Crystal Mountain, and the Manaslu Himal—are open! In the twenty-seven years since organized trekking began in Nepal, these fascinating regions were always tantalizingly close but unreachable. Before the days of trekking—the early 1960s—a twenty-five-mile restricted zone was created along the Nepal/Tibet border . . . At press time (June, 1992) the government of Nepal was finalizing the details to permit group trekking into each of these areas.[29]

I know the power of such rumors quite well. I've stood at the crumbling gate along the northern wall of Kagbeni village and looked up the sweep of the Kali Gandaki River draining the forbidden kingdom of Mustang, envious at the thought of going there. That was before the border region opened to Westerners and when the pastel landscape of the dry plateau country was still off-limits to foreigners. Kagbeni was the end of the tourist road in north central Nepal. It's the same old thing—we yearn to go where we know we cannot or should not, to have a peek at what's beyond the bend. The promise of delivery into virgin tourist land is what keeps the adventure agencies at the edge of travel.

The valued geography of the adventure destinations includes the attributes of remoteness and isolation—they are considered pre-requisites for authenticity, for unusual or especially aesthetic landscapes, for uncommon cultural traditions, and for the absence of contact with the modernized outside world that so greatly appeals to visitors from that same world. Foremost among the factors that shape the adventure places is how such destinations are (re)presented in the adventure travel literature and promotional brochures. InnerAsia Expeditions described its trekking program into the Turkish highlands thus:

> Here is Turkey at its most unexpected: dense evergreen for-
> ests, snow-streaked mountains, beds of wildflowers, nomads
> dancing to the music of bagpipes . . . The green terraces of
> the Pontic's lower slopes are reminiscent of Nepal, and the
> higher elevations are rather like a slightly muted Switzer-
> land.[30]

In telling it as something other than what we thought, and likening it to places other than itself, the passage conveys only an ambivalent and ambiguous view of what Turkey *is*. But it does impart a sense of mystery *about* Turkey. That, of all things, may be the strongest inspiration for the clients of a Turkish adventure.

Mystery, after all, is what most travelers seek and what the adventure tourists have come to expect. The trick apparently is to ensure that the mystery promised is the one delivered. Fortunately for the adventure agencies, that is not often difficult, given the nature of the places they visit. It is found easily in the shifting colors of a Muslim woman's *bourkha*, in the indecipherable speech of a foreign tongue, in the elaborate and repetitive rituals of priests of unfamiliar religions, in the inscrutable gaze of beggars, in the blowing of a conch shell, in the incessantly twisted shapes and patterns of shadows that play on the paved stones of unmarked alleys and at the portals of closed courtyard doors. Recognizing that geography may well be a matter of the mind, the Above the Clouds Trekking agency describes its itinerary to Peru:

Peru . . . just hearing the name brings to the imagination visions of high jungle trails passing through Incan ruins, magnificent monuments of a past era; icy peaks rising above myriad patchwork fields; raging torrents of glacier-fed rivers; the graceful flight of the condor; and the screeching cries of macaws passing overhead in the steamy jungles of the Amazon Basin area.[31]

Locating images outside of their geography is common in the tourism brochures, as is the selective editing of places to overlook that which may be undesirable. It is inevitable, perhaps, that the adventure tours restrict their coverage to the overlooks, since resolving them beyond that may show blemishes in such places. For instance, in its description of a tour to India's desert state of Rajasthan, Himalayan Travel tells its readers that in the great desert city of Jodhpur they will see the ancient Fort of Jodhpur, the old capital of Mandore, and the elaborate Hall of Heroes. They leave out of their description mention of the other sights of the city.

One year, a friend and I had several hours in Jodhpur before a train departure. We decided to visit the zoo, thinking that it might be a pleasant place and of some interest to us. We were directed by a passerby to a depressing site, dusty and barren, bound by barbed wire fencing. There was a small charge for entering. The first installation we came upon was a concrete and wire aviary filled with park pigeons and their considerable excrement. Although we were the only visitors in the zoo at the time, we hurried along to the next exhibit. There we saw a fenced area, bare of vegetation, surrounding a wooden box that measured less than two feet square. It was summer at that time, and I remember the heat was horrific. There was no sign of life anywhere in the enclosed area, but the small wooden container obviously was home to some creature. We wondered what might live in that box. There was no signboard to explain its contents, so we waited awhile to see what might emerge. After some time, a lean, gray house cat gingerly stepped out, stretched, looked around, pissed, and retreated to the dark interior of its home. We left the zoo immediately for the train station and shortly thereafter our train left Jodhpur for New Delhi. In the weeks prior to our Jodhpur zoo visit, we had met many Westerners on camel safari tours in the far desert near Jaisalmir, but we saw none of them at the zoo. Apparently, in the creation of Rajasthan as an adventure destination, no mention was made of Jodhpur's wildlife.

Despite this common temptation to create unblemished products, the adventure agencies may sometimes be quite forthright in explaining their role as designers of adventure tour products. For example, International Expeditions, Inc., listing its Southeast Asia tour, wrote:

> Start with the lure of Asia as exemplified by Thailand's rich culture and historic treasures; combine incredible wildlife, rain forest and island experiences in Borneo, mix in Taman Negara on Peninsular Malaysia and finish with ultra modern Singapore. If this is isn't enough, top it off with the most beautiful island on Earth—Bali—and you have the ingredi-

ents for one of the most exotic expeditions to be found anywhere.

For the past four years we have been testing and improving this expedition within our destination development process.[32]

The passage reads like a geographical stew and tells nothing about the places themselves. Since the choice of adventure destinations by prospective tour clients is highly dependent upon how they are shown by the adventure agencies, the creation of places as tourism products is an essential aspect of adventure travel. This production requires the formation of geographic impressions of places, a matter of some concern to us all since they shape our worlds. As it extends our images of world places to the very margins of the world system, where the periphery is both real and imagined, and as it connects the economies and societies of distant places with those of the core industrial countries that generate tourists, adventure travel becomes a major force of modernity. More than the sum of its innumerable impacts, it is this paramount achievement that defines tourism's compelling role in today's world.

5

Consequences of Discovery

In the summer of 1992, in Apia, Western Samoa, I boarded the Fijian cargo ship *Wairuwa*, bound for the Tokelau islands. My intention was to visit a country that was empty of tourists. Tokelau seemed a good bet. It consists of three tiny coral island clusters situated a few degrees latitude south of the equator and 480 kilometers north of Western Samoa, its closest large neighbor. The total land area of Tokelau is a meager twelve square kilometers, fragmented into over 125 islets, none of them reaching more than five meters above the level of the surrounding sea. This lack of height is a concern for some islanders: Tokelau has the dubious distinction of being the first nation that will go underwater in the event of the sea level rise associated with the global warming predictions. The islets, in addition to being low-lying, are incredibly narrow; the distance from outer sea to inner lagoon across the sward of coral sand is often less than one hundred meters; the fronts of many homes face the pounding ocean while the backyards open onto the quiet eddies of the interior lagoons.

During hurricanes, which happen altogether too frequently—the worst occurring in 1846, 1914, 1966, 1987, and 1990—the seas rush inward to cover the land, washing away gardens, pigs, and homes. Tokelau, washed by the seas and ringed by the vastness of the Pacific, seems as evanescent as the ocean swells themselves. It's hard to imagine a place that is more remote and at a world scale more geographically insignificant than Tokelau. One measure of its disjunction with the world is the lack of tourists who visit there.

In 1991, the island population was only seventeen hundred, but over twice that many Tokelauans live abroad, mainly in New Zealand. There are several times more pigs than people in Tokelau, and fifteen times more lagoon area than land. No air link exists in the islands. Until 1993, the *Wairuwa* was the sole way to reach Tokelau, and it made the journey once a month as it completed a large trading circuit that took the vessel between Fiji, Rotuma, Samoa, the northern Cook Islands, and Tokelau. Some months, the vessel never arrived at all. Tokelau is now serviced by the *Cape Don* and the *Salamasena*, which together provide more reliable service.

Before the *Wairuwa* started visiting the islands, there was no regular ship service and the last vessel that traded with Tokelau simply disappeared one year with everyone aboard. When I visited Tokelau in the summer of 1992, only half a dozen other Westerners had gone to the islands that year; most of them were New Zealanders on government missions. One of the other visitors, a ham radio operator from Chatham Island, New Zealand, had lived on Nukunonu Atoll for several months prior to my arrival, and was catching a return ride to Apia aboard the *Wairuwa*. Apparently, atmospheric energy circulations were bent that year such that Tokelau was situated to receive excellent long-range transmissions. The New Zealand radio man, in addition to conducting his studies of earth magnetism, could talk to his buddies living on all the continents on earth.

There is no policy in Tokelau to manage tourism, and few tourists go there. Tokelau, in fact, may be one of the few countries in the world that does *not* have a tourism agenda. Most islanders still enjoy a subsistence lifestyle that is typical of traditional Polynesia: they fish, keep pigs, and tend small gardens. With most of its population living abroad, considerable foreign exchange enters Tokelau in the form of remittances sent by workers in New Zealand

to their families living on the islands. In 1991, the remittances amounted to 120 New Zealand dollars for every islander—a considerable sum since there is very little to buy. An additional 380 dollars per person comes from selling postage stamps and sea-shells—the main exports of Tokelau, besides the copra and dried fish. Most of the large development projects in Tokelau—water systems, generators, housing—are financed by the New Zealand government.' With such considerable outside economic intervention already, Tokelau sees little need for tourism.

If all that paints a fairly rosy picture, it is diminished by the changes that such economic arrangements have produced for island lifestyles. Tokelau is now locked into a dependency upon New Zealand assistance and the remittances from abroad. Income and education disparities divide the population. Traditional knowledge is becoming obsolete, values are breaking down, diets are changing. An older man said that nowadays, since young islanders own outboard motorboats, few learn about the weather and the reef behavior of fish—they think that since they can get around faster, they can make mistakes. The average Tokelauan consumes one kilogram of sugar each week and almost three kilograms of tobacco per year. No figures on beer consumption were available, but my own survey of the cargo hold of the *Wairuwa* en route to Tokelau tells me that Kiwi Lager from New Zealand must surpass most other imports. Card-playing and beer-drinking appear to be the major pastimes for island residents. Tokelau, despite its outward tranquillity, is no paradise for many of its inhabitants.

When we left the wharf at Apia, the *Wairuwa* was scheduled to make a seven-day swing through the three Tokelau atolls—Faka'ofo, Nukunonu, and Atafu, before returning to Apia. The vessel, owned by the island of Rotuma—an outlier of the Fiji Island group, and crewed by sturdy Fijians—is an iron-clad, six-hundred-ton ship with a chipped green coat, a large cargo hold, and deck space for one hundred island passengers. It was a sailor's ship, greasy, dirty, functional. The only decorative item I found on board was a faded picture of snow-capped Mount Cook in New Zealand's southern Alps. It hung awkwardly on a cabin wall next to a poster showing step-by-step instructions of what to do in the event of a sinking ship.

On that trip, as I suspect was the case on all trips to Tokelau, every conceivable spot on deck was taken by islanders sprawled on mats and surrounded by their assorted belongings. They were returning from extended overseas stays, from shopping trips to Apia, from family visits abroad, from classes at one of the Pacific regional colleges. For a small population, the Tokelauans travel a great deal; apparently, although Tokelau accepts few tourists, the islanders frequently are tourists themselves. For the entire week aboard ship, everyone was either asleep, singing, eating, or playing cards. Each day the passengers were served a meat stew and white bread from the ship's galley. That was augmented by whatever food the passengers happened to bring along with them.

It was hardly a luxury cruise, and it was clear to me, regardless of any official policy that Tokelau had toward restricting tourism, that the *Wairuwa* simply was not an option for getting tourists to the islands. The atolls, too, had no place for visitors. Not a single hotel or restaurant exists in Tokelau. No handicrafts are for sale, either. Nothing but coral sand beaches and crystal lagoons, breaking waves, coconut palms, and colorful village homes. The setting, indeed, was authentic, but by its very authenticity, it precluded tourists.

Wherever the *Wairuwa* stopped to unload cargo, I went ashore. Small outboards pulled alongside the moving ship and any disembarking passengers had to jump onto the smaller boats and then ride through the fringing reef to shore. I found the main island of the southernmost cluster, Faka'ofo, to be overcrowded, with everyone living on one small islet in tight wooden houses with tin roofs. Faka'ofo hosts the Tokelauan government offices, a school and dispensary, a tin storage shed for supplies, and over seventy-six motorboats. The most notable features were the seaweed-eating

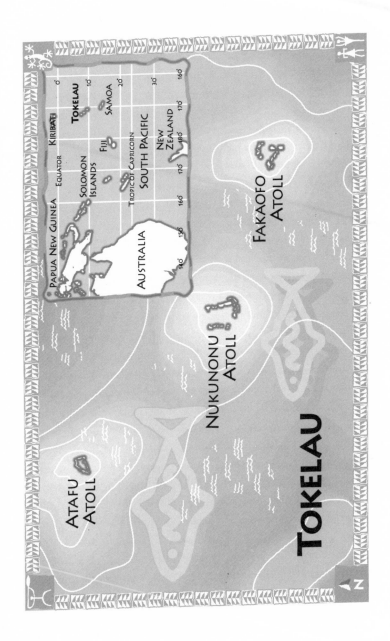

and ocean-swimming pigs that rummaged the reefs at low tide. The islets on the far side of the lagoon, well beyond Faka'ofo village, were uninhabited except for occasional copra workers and fishermen.

The middle atoll, Nukunonu, ringed the largest lagoon in Tokelau. Most compelling were its waters, which contained all the shades of blue and green as they dissolved into the white coral islets on the horizon. Nukunonu is less densely populated than Faka'ofo, and for that reason alone was a more pleasant place to stay.

The northernmost atoll is Atafu. It also is the loveliest atoll in the Tokelau group, its communities the best kept, and its people perhaps the most industrious that I saw in Tokelau. At Atafu, more than on any of the other atolls, I saw the way island subsistence life can work. The traditional stitched wooden outriggers are used still for fishing in the lagoon. Each home has a small garden kept fertile by compost and careful tending. Breadfruit trees, swamp taro, papayas, bananas, and coconuts supplement the steady diet of seafood—reef fishes such as goatfish, garfish, and surgeonfish, and deepwater tuna and shark. Sea and land are inextricably linked in the way islanders have adapted culturally to that small place.

The traditional patterns that survive in Tokelau, especially on Atafu Atoll, show how such people are vertically linked to their place, grounded in its history, and tied to its future. In that way, the Pacific islanders differ little from other native peoples. Ecological relationships, and the social organizations that maintain them, define the way subsistence people everywhere gather and use natural resources. Culture is not a show but a means of survival. The local environment is not an ecological theater but the chief means of making a living. The way resources are known and used, the methods of obtaining them, and the social formations that govern the distribution of them, all shape the vertical axis of subsistence life which anchors people in the traditions and the productivity of the place in which they live.

Just as in Tokelau, where the regular overseas remittances and the international migrations extend the islanders' world across half an ocean, new modernization trends everywhere extend the vertical linkages of people beyond their immediate environments. People do not live in isolation, even in such remote places as Tokelau. New horizontal linkages form the arteries that connect people and local places with the wider world. Modernity has arrived everywhere, and the linkages it establishes take various shapes. With the exception of minor places such as Tokelau, foremost among these new linkages is tourism.

Tourism has eclipsed traditional industries worldwide to generate over 55 billion dollars annually, accounting for 25 percent of international trade in services and 12 percent of the world gross product. The rapid expansion of tourism is most notable in its specialized segments such as adventure travel. While government agencies and private industries commonly track the statistical record of tourism, the nature of its impacts generally escape the scrutiny of the accounting measures. Geographers, anthropologists, and other social scientists have only recently begun to study how tourism shapes cultures and societies. Valene Smith sees the tourism impacts as being the products of the "exchanges" that occur between the tourists, who act as guests, and the local people who serve as their hosts.[2] The consequences of tourism discovery extend, however, beyond the individual economic transactions and the cultural changes that occur as a result of the interaction between tourists and hosts. Tourism interacts with *places*, and in so doing it establishes entirely new identities for them, for the people who live in them, and for those who visit them. That is most notable in those distant places on earth that, until the recent interests in ecotourism, ethnic tourism, and other forms of adventure travel, have maintained a strong connection with their pasts.

The new forms of adventure tourism establish new tourist paths, movements to new places, new spaces, where all roads lead to some kind of shrine (the Sacred Way). At its best, to paraphrase Samuel Johnson, travel regulates the imagination by reality, and instead of imagining how things may be, sees them as they are. But know, too, that Hermes, the Greek god of roads and travelers, was the protector of all entrances—including that of Hades. As the journeys of tourism combine the imagined and the real, much of what we know about the world comes from first hand experience. This is true for people who never leave a place as well as for those who never settle down. Somewhere in between the two extremes are the travelers and the tourists. They temporarily leave the worlds of their making, to remake the places they visit. We are, it seems, continually returning to ourselves, but never unchanged. So, too, the places that tourists visit are always becoming something new: the end of the road is also the beginning.

Travelers often are exalted, but tourists are quickly dismissed, as nuisances, and more malignantly as destroyers. Mark Twain, in his book *Innocents Abroad*, called them "incorrigible pilgrims" and "invading tribes." Some places, such as Tokelau, do not encourage them to visit. A few other countries greatly restrict their numbers and activities. Most places, however, are willing to "give the devil his due," and have plunged heartily into the investment prospects of tourism development. The economic interests of tourism have conveniently centered on the roles of mass tourism and destination resorts.

Those interests are tied to the broader issues of economic development. There is little reason to see tourism as distinct from the rest of development: the capital outlays required to build the mega-hotels, the infrastructure required to transport and service the 400 million people who tour internationally each year, the tremendous revenues that are generated, all fail to distinguish tourism from the other forms of modern industrial development.[3] Nowadays, however, with tourists moving beyond the built environments of the conventional destinations, on to the remote places that have little tourism infrastructure and practically no experience dealing with tourism, the issue is not one exclusively of economic development, but of the construction of places, identities, and imaginations. Where early travel construed the narrative of a slow journey among traditional places, modern adventure tourism constructs a new narrative of old places *becoming modern.*

The optimism of the modern world and our disillusionment with it are what propel adventure tourism into the world's most inaccessible reaches. There, tourists confront rhythms that are distinctly different from the pace of life found in the West. In attempting to fuse the modern and the "primitive," tourism fails miserably. Perhaps that may be due to bad timing. Much of the impetus for adventure travel lies in its attempts to seek out places that show older times and ways of living, attempts really to recapture a past lost to the quickness of modernity. Marshall Berman wrote in his book *All That Is Solid Melts into Air:*

> . . . our past, whatever it was, was a past in the process of disintegration; we yearn to grasp it, but it is baseless and elusive; we look back for something solid to lean on, only to find ourselves embracing ghosts.[4]

But to bring to old and slower places the speed of the modern Western world is to introduce to those places the incongruities that many Western tourists experience when they try to reconcile an organic, considered way of living with the techno-industrial basis that supports our material life. The two often grind against one another, like jamming the gearbox of an automobile from first into fourth gear. Gary Snyder relates an amusing incident that occurred during his visit among aborigines in central Australia:

> We were traveling by truck over dirt track west from Alice Springs in the company of a Pintubi elder named Jimmy Tjungurrayi. As we rolled along the dusty road, sitting in the bed of a pickup, he began to speak very rapidly to me. He

was talking about a mountain over there, telling me a story about some wallabies that came to that mountain in the dreamtime and got into some kind of mischief with some lizard girls. He had hardly finished that and he started in on another story about another hill over here and another story over there. I couldn't keep up. I realized after about half an hour of this that these were tales to be told while *walking*, and I was experiencing a speeded-up version of what might be leisurely told over several days of foot travel.[5]

The paradox of modern adventure tourism lies in the fact that as it connects remote communities to wider regions by circulating people, goods, and money through the traditional economies, it makes those places less attractive for subsequent adventure tours. Clearly, such a way of operating is not sustainable. It is only a matter of time before places become too commercialized for adventure purposes and are abandoned by the adventure agencies. At that point, the tourism product changes to one that appeals to less adventurous people, and pretty soon the place becomes simply another fabricated tourism spot enjoyed by ordinary holidaymakers. Such places readily become an accumulation of the economic transactions and social exchanges that are tied to tourism, and they lose their identity in the bargain; they become commonplace.

The speed with which such changes occur can be remarkable. Tourists, especially adventure tourists, are keen to this and forever seek to visit a place "before it is discovered and ruined." For those same tourists to think they can somehow remove themselves from the process of ruination shows the power of the imagination—as if they could slip into and out of a place unnoticed. This shows in Thailand, where the tourists who avoid the hill tribe regions in the north travel instead to the islands in the south. By the late 1970s, the southern destinations remained obscure places, offering for tourists a few simple huts for lodging and local food, empty beaches, and plenty of clear ocean water. Today, those same islands, places such as Phi Phi Island, Ko Samui, and Phuket, are overrun with mass tourists, restaurants, speedboats, nightclubs, and high-rise hotels. The southbound adventure tourists have moved on to such alternative places as Ko Samet island, where the beach bungalows largely remain unlighted and the best thing still to do at night is watch the stars. Even there, the grip of tourism has taken hold: in 1990, new signboards announced the imminent construction of new hotels, windsurfing lessons were offered at a local restaurant, and in at least one of the new restaurants near the boat launch the night air reverberated with video tracks.

In Morocco, where European tourists on a short holiday contend with overland travelers on long trans-African journeys, the distinction between the two is a matter of space as well as time. Coastal cities such as Tangier and Casablanca attract the tourists with the five-star hotels, beaches, belly-dances, and shopping lanes. The number of tourists drops off with increasing distance from the coast, leaving much of the Atlas Mountains and the interior desert to themselves and to the long-term travelers. Paul Bowles set his book *The Sheltering Sky* in Morocco. It is a story of travelers, but the protagonist is the desert: the people who attempt to journey into it find themselves traveling mainly into themselves. Such a journey cannot be attained on a short-lived tour: "He did not think of himself as a tourist; he was a traveler. The difference is partly one of time, he would explain."[6]

In the interior of Morocco lies the desert town of Marrakech, a labyrinth of walled compounds, gates, and narrow lanes of shops and homes. In the center of the town is the huge *medina* where the traders and merchants, water-carriers, and hucksters all congregate. Outside the fortress walls of the town is a fenced campground for Western travelers. You find there people sleeping in tents, on the ground in sleeping bags, in camper vans, on the beds of massive overlander trucks. In the morning, people bathe at the few water spigots, wash clothes and hang them to dry in the sun, and ready themselves for the walk into town. Throughout the day the grounds remain empty, but around dusk they fill again with the returning travelers. Outside the clearly defined perimeter of the fenced area, local Moroccans sit or stand idly in small groups: their sole interest is watching the tourists. Hucksters call into the campground with prices for handicrafts. Tour operators announce the next day's itinerary.

The smell of hashish permeates the air around the campground. The tourists who stay there are on display. The roles have been reversed, where the knickknacks, the ways of brushing teeth, the peculiar languages, the hairstyles and clothing designs of the Western visitors are the amusement of their hosts. It is disconcerting to be gazed at inscrutably for hours at a time, like a caged animal in a zoo. Yet that is what much of tourism, especially the so-called ethnic tourism, is about. I imagine that what people who live in the tourist places feel most deeply is that loss of privacy—and the abrogation of control they have over the intimate parts of their lives.

I experienced a situation somewhat similar to the Moroccan campground several years later in Nepal. A man I know, a village priest with idle time, lives in a small thatch hut in the Marsyangdi Valley along one of the main trekking circuits heading north around Annapurna. His home is perched a small way above the trail. Every day during the trekking season he watches the parade of Westerners hiking up and down the path below his house. The tourists, with their colorful outfits, space-age backpacks, and two-hundred-dollar boots, offer a strange sight on the Himalaya road, and provide my friend, who watches them much as one might follow the passage of migrating birds or colorful sailboats in a race, with a considerable amount of casual entertainment. Not content to watch, my elderly friend would try to guess, with amazing alacrity, the various nationalities of the trekkers. He would yell out his choice, so that broken bits of "HEY, GERMANY!" or "AUSTRALIAN!" or "MONSIEUR FRANCE!" rained down on the hikers from the small hut above. For my friend, it was the tourists from throughout the world who provided the amusement, while he kept out of sight.

Tourist places are always in the process of *becoming modern*, but mainly at the behest of visitors for whom they simply paint a pretty picture. Their "modernity" is a falsehood of misconstrued imagery, rather than a logical extension of their own histories. The construction of Western modernity is one of a progression through various economies—from the extraction of primary resources, through the secondary sector of manufacturing, and on to the tertiary economies that mainly provide services. The most advanced nations currently grapple with their new identities derived from a fourth form of economy—creating, assembling, and disseminating information. Places turned over to tourism leap from the primary to the tertiary levels of economic transactions, bypassing the factories, and then move quickly on to the fourth sector, where their very identity is tied to what tourists know about them. In such a rapid move, things become less dependable. The old ways of living are not sustained, but new alternatives are not always forthcoming. The potential for conflict exists between a life based upon a reliable past and one that is designed by an unknown future.

Knowing that such situations confront them, some developing countries have established comprehensive plans to make the touristic use of natural and cultural resources more sustainable, and to commit tourism to a long-term investment in the places it frequents. Quite often, those plans call for the creation of national parklands and preserves. Advocates of adventure tourism propose that its primary contribution to the Third World is in helping to establish the awareness and the financial support necessary for the development of national parks in locations where they might not otherwise occur. The argument for park development in the developing countries emphasizes their economic value. That is understandable since the top priority of those countries is economic development.

There is a risk to such an evaluation. According to international parks expert John Blower:

Governments, especially in poorer countries, tend understandably to be interested primarily in development projects with prospects of early economic return, preferably in the form of much-needed foreign exchange. It is therefore natural in endeavoring to "sell" the idea of national parks to a possibly unenthusiastic government to stress their potential as tourist attractions. There are, however, dangers in this since it is likely to lead to the assumption by decision-makers that parks exist primarily for economic gain, with the corollary that if their expectations in this direction are not fulfilled the planners may begin to look for more profitable alternative uses for lands . . . thus destroying the parks' wilderness values and eventually turning them into areas of which the main objective is mass tourism rather than conservation.[7]

The model for national parks in Third World countries originated in North America, beginning with Yellowstone National Park, in which natural areas were set aside to combine the interests of environmental protection and recreational use. But the historical contexts between new and proposed Third World parks and the already established North American parks are quite different. The validation of parks in North American society links historically to evolving perspectives on the very idea of wilderness.

Early North American history rests on the premise that European cultural expansion onto the western frontier was necessary. According to historian J. Frederick Turner, the need to "tame" the wilderness in the American West is what imparted to the American character such qualities as resoluteness and resiliency. In the early twentieth century, a "wilderness cult" developed within certain segments of American intellectual and social life, prompted by poets, artists, and scientists, which attributed to wilderness parks the opportunities for aesthetic and spiritual renewal, as well as environmental protection. Notably absent from the North American parks were the indigenous people of the North American landscape; the Native American Indians had been eliminated or displaced to reservations long before the government proclamations that created the parks became law.

In the developing countries, there has been no similar history of an institutional "wilderness ethic" per se, although the native people, living in the local ecosytems, have developed highly complex ways of thinking about and living in the wild world. Furthermore, the frontier regions of the developing countries, areas designated for park development, are precisely those places where indigenous people now live. They *own* such places by rights of tradition, and the advent of tourism onto their lands connects their local interests with those of national governments. Such places integrate the often contradictory aims of governments, tourists, and native people. The strategy has appeal, since today over three thousand such areas are established in over 120 countries. Most, if not all, of the spots designated as protected areas have about them a tourism component. As they extend the geographical range of adventure tourism, it remains unclear what such parks are protected from.

Presumably, natural environments that contain significant numbers of threatened plant and animal species need protecting from the ravages of logging, dams, mining, and other extractive industries, and the indigenous cultures that occupy the frontier areas may, indeed, need protection from the "corruption" of outside societies. By setting aside the former as nature preserves, we may well safeguard the flora and fauna that dwell within. But to maintain cultural territories as "parks" raises the question of "human zoos," and uncovers the sad history of Native American Indian reservations in the United States, tribal "homelands" in South Africa, sedentary camps for Tibetan nomads, and other similarly botched attempts at managing human preserves. Adventure travel is the latest incursion into the world refuges of jungles, deserts, islands, and mountains. Its impacts are considerable. Many people spend their professional careers debating the pros and the cons of tourism, weighing the balance, and striving for some clarity about it. In my experience, the overriding concern of tourism is one of authenticity—not so much of the places that tourists visit, but rather of tourism itself—how it offers itself and the integrity that it maintains as a major social and economic force. As it draws the remote frontiers of the world into the global economy, adventure travel emboldens conservation groups with the weighty argument of economics, it entices the national governments of developing countries with the prospect of foreign earnings, it placates the indigenous people whose territory it invades by letting them think that they will retain control over their own lives, and it flim-flams the tourists by selling a mere holiday as an adventure. In its attempt to make travelers out of tourists, but offering only destinations and no journey, adventure tourism falls short. But by packaging cultures and natural places into itineraries, adventure tourism succeeds well at selling illusions. Most of the time, that is good enough.

> We knew we were in another world when on the last day of the trek one of our guides went off in native costume with bow and arrow—to fight in a tribal war! Papua New Guinea was fascinating![8]

Notes

1. Tourist Trails

1. For discussions of international tourism, its impacts, and its role in world development, see E. de Kadt, *Tourism: Passport to Development?* (Oxford: Oxford University Press, 1979); and A. Mathieson and G. Wall, *Tourism: Economic, Physical, and Social Impacts* (London: Longman, 1982).

2. R. Butler, "Alternative Tourism: Pious Hope or Trojan Horse?" *Journal of Travel Research* 28/3 (1990): 40–45. See also L. Richter, "The Search for Appropriate Tourism," *Tourism Recreation Research* 12/2 (1987): 5–7.

3. Hector Caballos-Lascuria, "Tourism, Ecotourism, and Protected Areas" (Paper presented at the Second International Symposium on Ecotourism, Miami, Fla., 27 November–2 December 1990).

4. J. Kusler, "Ecotourism and Resource Conservation: An Introduction to Issues," and M. Passoff, "Ecotourism Re-Examined" (Papers presented at Second International Symposium on Ecotourism, Miami, Fla., 27 November–2 December 1990).

5. Tensie Whelan, *Nature Tourism: Managing for the Environment* (Washington, D.C.: Island Press, 1991).

6. For example, meetings include two international symposia on ecotourism (Merida, 1989; Miami, 1990); Banff Seminar on Tourism: Find the Balance (1990); World Congress on Adventure Travel (Manaus, forthcoming); Design Workshop: Ecotourism Resort Development, U.S. Virgin Islands (1991). Publications include *Ecotourism and Resource Conservation* (two volumes edited by J. Kusler; proceedings of two international symposia); Elizabeth Boo, *Ecotourism: Potential and Pitfalls* (World Wildlife Fund); Karen Ziffer, *Eco-Tourism: The Uneasy Alliance* (The

Ecotourism Society). Organizations include The Ecotourism Society (Bennington, Vt.); Blue Peace Pacific (Sydney); Center for Responsible Tourism (San Anselmo, Calif.); Tourism with Insight (*Tourismus mit Einsicht*; Berlin).

7. Linda Richter, "The Search for Appropriate Tourism," *Tourism Recreation Research* 12/2 (1987): 5–7.

8. From George Doubleday's frontispiece letter to prospective clients in the 1990 InnerAsia Expeditions brochure. InnerAsia Expeditions, 2627 Lombard Street, San Francisco, CA 94123. The emphasis on *travel* rather than *tourism* is common to most of the appeals found in the adventure agency brochures.

9. S. Graham, *Adventure Travel in Latin America* (Berkeley, Calif.: Wilderness Press, 1990), 1.

10. C. Rajendra, "When the Tourists Flew in," *Contours* 1/4 (1983): 9. Quoted in L. Richter, *The Politics of Tourism in Asia* (Honolulu: University of Hawaii Press, 1989).

11. P. Deardon, "Tourism and Sustainable Development in Northern Thailand," *Geographical Review* 81/4 (1991): 400–413.

12. See for example M. Redclift, *Sustainable Development: Exploring the Contradictions* (London: Methuen, 1987); A. Yo, *Social Change and Development: Modernization, Dependency, and World-Systems Theory* (Newbury Park, Calif.: Sage Publications, Inc., 1990).

13. J. Lea, *Tourism Development in the Third World* (London: Routledge, 1988): 2.

14. Butler, "Alternative Tourism." See also P. Gonsalves, "Alternative Tourism—the Evolution of a Network," *Tourism Recreation Research* 12/2 (1987): 9–12. A network of alternative tourism advocates exists worldwide and includes: The Center for Responsible Tourism (San Anselmo, Calif.); the Ecumenical Coalition on Third World Tourism (Bangalore, India); and Tourism with Insight group (Berlin, Germany).

15. L. Turner and J. Ash, *The Golden Hordes: International Tourism and the Pleasure Periphery* (London: Constable, 1975).

16. S. Britton, "The Political Economy of Tourism in the Third World," *Annals of Tourism Research* 9/3 (1982): 331–358.

17. B. Farrell, *Hawaii: The Legend That Sells* (Honolulu: University of Hawaii Press, 1982).

18. S. Britton, "The Spatial Organization of Tourism in a Neocolonial Economy: A Fijian Case Study," *Pacific Viewpoints* 21/2 (1980): 144–165.

19. S. Pearsall and W. Whistler, *Terrestrial Ecosystem Mapping for Western Samoa: Summary, Project Report, and Proposed National Parks and Reserves Plan* (Apia: South Pacific Regional Environment Program [SPREP] and Honolulu: East-West Center, Environment and Policy Institute, 1991).

20. The *Adventure Travel Society Newsletter*, Fall 1992.

21. The economic determination of wilderness resources as tourism resources is used to argue against wildlife and wildlands destruction from commercial over-exploitation, extractive government policies, and poaching. See K. Lindberg, *Policies for Maximizing Nature Tourism's Ecological and Economic Benefits* (Washington, D.C.: World Resources Institute, 1991).

22. Elizabeth Boo, *Ecotourism: The Potentials and Pitfalls*, 2 vols. (Washington, D.C.: World Wildlife Fund, 1990).

23. For an extensive discussion of hill to tarai migration in Nepal and the problems of landlessness in the lowlands, see N. Shrestha, *Landlessness and Migration in Nepal* (Boulder: Westview Press, 1990).

24. R. Butler,"The Concept of Tourist Area Cycle of Evolution: Implications for Management of Resources," *The Canadian Geographer* 24 (1980): 5–12.

2. Along the Way

1. Edward W. Said, *Orientalism* (New York: Pantheon Books, 1978), 4–5.

1. Ibid.

3. Linda Nochlin, *The Politics of Vision: Essays on Nineteenth-Century Art and Society* (New York: Harper and Row Publishers, 1989), 50. For additional critiques on vision and art, see also J. Berger, *Ways of Seeing* (London: BBC; Harmondsworth: Penguin, 1974); J. Berger, *About Looking* (New York: Pantheon Books, 1980); and S. Sontag, *On Photography* (New York: Farrar, Straus and Giroux, 1977).

4. Nochlin, *The Politics of Vision*, 50.

5. Rudyard Kipling, "The Man Who Would Be King," in *The Phantom Rickshaw and Other Stories* (New York: J. H. Sears and Company, 1925), 172.

6. Mary Louis Pratt, *Imperial Eyes: Travel Writing and Transculturation* (London: Routledge, 1992), 18.

7. Joseph P. Ferrier, "Caravans, Journeys, and Wanderings," in *Travel and Travelers of the Middle Ages*, ed. A. P. Newton (Freeport, N.Y.: Books for Library Press, 1967).

8. Erik Cohen, "Alternative Tourism—A Critique," *Tourism Recreation*

Research 12/2 (1987): 14. Other attempts to categorize tourists classify them according to their location on a psychocentric continuum—from the self-inhibited traveler to the outgoing adventurer, each of whom produces unique travel activities and patterns; see also S. C. Plog, "Why Destination Areas Rise and Fall in Popularity," *Cornell Hotel and Restaurant Association Quarterly*, February 1974, 55–58.

9. Joseph Conrad, "The Heart of Darkness," in *Youth and Two Other Stories* (Garden City, N.Y.: Doubleday, 1925), 52.

10. For a personal summary of his life of exploration, see Sven Hedin, *My Life as an Explorer* (Garden City, N.Y.: Garden City Publishing Co., 1925).

11. Peter Bishop, *The Myth of Shangri-La: Tibet, Travel Writing, and the Western Creation of a Sacred Landscape* (Berkeley: University of California Press, 1989), 3.

12. For a series of essays that examine, in various cultural and geographical contexts, the production of the sense of place, see J. Agnew and J. Duncan, eds., *The Power of Place: Bringing Together Geographical and Sociological Imaginations* (Boston: Unwin and Hyman, 1989).

13. Bishop, *The Myth of Shangri-La*, 4. Bishop's analysis relies primarily on historical written narratives. His ideas on how travel routes are created link equally well to oral accounts and anecdotes shared by travelers along the road.

14. The idea of tourists' relationship to the landscapes they visit lacks much attention in critical tourism literature. In travel literature, it maintains an appearance as reflective narration. In a bold attempt to analyze the symbolic content of a North American natural and tourism landscape—the Dakota Badlands—Elise Broach places the tourist squarely within it, to discover that "A landscape remade by humans can in turn remake those humans" (15). E. Broach, "Angels, Architect, and Erosion: The Dakota Badlands as Cultural Symbol," *North Dakota History* 59/1 (1992): 2–15.

15. P. Porter and F. Lukermann, "The Geography of Utopia," in *Geographies of the Mind: Essays in Historical Geosophy*, ed. D. Lowenthal and M. J. Bowden (New York: Oxford University Press, 1975), 199.

16. A. Falk, "Border Symbolism Revisited," in *Maps from the Mind: Readings in Psychogeography*, ed. H. Stein and W. G. Niederland (Norman: Oklahoma University Press, 1989), 156.

17. J. Allen, "Imagination and Geographical Exploration," in *Geographies of the Mind*, ed. Lowenthal and Bowden, 57.

18. Yi Fu Tuan, *Topophilia: A Study of Environmental Perceptions, Attitudes, and Values* (Englewood Cliffs, N.J.: Prentice-Hall, 1974). Refer also to J. D. Porteus, *Landscapes of the Mind: Worlds of Sense and Metaphor* (Toronto: University of Toronto Press, 1990).

19. The importance of Balkh as the center of ancient Bactria is shown by numerous archaeological excavations into Afghanistan's past. The archaeological effort, spanning several decades, records Afghanistan's pivotal role in the early history of central Asia. For a detailed assessment of the major findings, see F. R. Allchin and N. Hammond, eds., *The Archaeology of Afghanistan: From Earliest Times to the Timurid Period* (London: Academic Press, 1978). An account of Afghanistan's more recent history appears in A. Fletcher, *Afghanistan: Highway of Conquest* (Ithaca, N.Y.: Cornell University Press, 1965).

20. Louis Dupree, *Afghanistan* (Princeton, N.J.: Princeton University Press, 1973), 301.

21. Yi Fu Tuan, *Topophilia*, 4, 93.

22. For various accounts of the battles and the intrigues that surround the legendary history of the Khyber Pass, see Dupree, *Afghanistan*; Fletcher, *Afghanistan: Highway of Conquest*; and C. Miller, *Khyber: British India's Northwest Frontier* (New York: MacMillan Publishing Co., 1977).

23. Mark Twain, *Following the Equator*, vol. 2 (New York: Harper and Brothers, 1899), 26.

24. Linda Richter, *The Politics of Tourism in Asia* (Honolulu: University of Hawaii Press, 1989), 108.

25. Ibid., 117.

26. For a thorough explication of India's pre-Mogul history, see A. L. Basham, *The Wonder That Was India* (New York: Hawthorn Books, 1963).

27. V. S. Naipaul, *India: A Wounded Civilization* (New York: Alfred A. Knopf, 1977), 20.

28. Ibid.

29. Twain, *Following the Equator*, vol. 2, 35.

30. R. K. Narayan, *The Vendor of Sweets* (New York: Viking Penguin, 1983). Other books by Narayan that center on the metaphorical village of Malgudi include *Malgudi Days* (New York: Viking Penguin, 1985); *The Guide* (New York: Viking Penguin, 1992); *The Man-Eater of Malgudi* (New York: Viking Penguin, 1983).

31. For a splendid short exposé of Goa, see Ved Mehta, *Portrait of India* (New York: Farrar, Straus and Giroux, 1969), 442–447.

3. By All Means

1. Claude Lévi-Strauss, *Triste Tropiques* (New York: Atheneum, 1974), 37–38. The dean of structural anthropology wrote this book as a sort of memoir to recount personal reflections on decades of his path-breaking anthropology in various world places. An important theme in *Triste Tropiques* is the assimilation of cultures by Western models of modernization.

2. Ibid., 38.

3. This passage appears in a recent brochure of the Above the Clouds Trekking agency as part of Director Conlon's appeal to prospective clients. Quoted in David Zurick, "Adventure Travel and Sustainable Tourism in the Peripheral Economy of Nepal," *Annals of the Association of American Geographers* 82/4 (1992): 614.

4. Information on upcoming Adventure Travel Congresses and copies of congress proceedings can be obtained from The Adventure Travel Society, 6551 South Revere Parkway, Suite 160, Englewood, CO 80111.

5. S. Zukin, *Landscapes of Power: From Detroit to Disneyland* (Berkeley: University of California Press, 1991), especially 217–250. See also A. Wilson, *The Culture of Nature: From Disney to Exxon Valdez* (Cambridge, Mass.: Blackwell, 1992).

6. "Introduction," by Jerry Mallett, president of the Adventure Travel Society, in *Proceedings of the 1991 World Congress on Adventure Travel and Ecotourism* (Colorado Springs, Col., August 28–31, 1991), 2.

7. Ibid., 2. See also *Proceedings of the 1992 World Congress on Adventure Travel and Ecotourism* (Whistler, British Columbia, Sept. 20–23, 1992).

8. Paul Fussell, *Abroad: British Literary Traveling between the Wars* (New York: Oxford University Press, 1980), 39.

9. Nicholas Sullivan, "The President's Page," *The Explorers Journal* 68/1 (1990): 2. Note: the current president of The Explorers Club is David Swansen.

10. Christina Dodwell, *An Explorer's Handbook: An Unconventional Guide for Travelers to Remote Regions* (New York: Facts on File Publications, 1986), 51.

11. Joseph Campbell, "The Hero's Adventure," in *The Power of Myth* (New York: Doubleday, 1988), 123.

12. Graham Greene, *Journey without Maps* (New York: The Viking Press, 1965), 308–309.

13. Ibid., 310.

14. Joseph Campbell, *The Hero's Journey: The World of Joseph Campbell* (San Francisco: Harper and Row Publishers, 1990), vi.

15. Paul Bowles, *Their Heads Are Green and Their Hands Are Blue* (New York: Random House, 1963), 58.

16. The words are from an inscription dated A.D. 1292. Quoted in D. K. Syatt, *Thailand: A Short History* (New Haven and London: Yale University Press, 1984), 54.

17. Phil Dearden, "Tourism and Sustainable Development in Northern Thailand," *Geographical Review* 81/4 (1991): 400–413. His estimate was based on a sampling of Western trekkers in which he found that 5 percent paid an average twenty-nine baht (Thailand currency) total for photographs. See p. 407 of his article for computations.

18. Ibid.

19. Jerry Mallett, "1993 Outlook for Adventure Travel," in *1993 Outlook for Travel and Tourism* (Washington, D.C.: United States Travel Data Center, 1993), 157.

20. Ibid., 158.

21. *Wilderness Travel Catalogue*, 1992 (Wilderness Travel, 801 Allston Way, Berkeley, CA 94710), 4.

22. Ibid., 5.

23. Robert Harbison, *Eccentric Spaces: A Voyage through Real and Imagined Worlds* (Boston: David R. Godine Publisher, 1988).

24. "Indiana Jones, Say Hi to Ralph Lauren," *New York Times*, 21 December 1992, Travel Section. The Sunday editions of major urban newspapers frequently contain travel accounts of the various adventure packages organized worldwide—this media attention is a good measure of adventure travel's current popularity.

25. Josiah Tucker, *Instructions for Travelers* (Yorkshire, England: S. R. Publishers, Ltd., 1757), 3.

26. Ibid., 4.

27. Quoted in R. S. Lambert, ed., *Grand Tour: A Journey in the Tracks of Aristocracy* (New York: E. P. Dutton and Company, 1937), 29. See also F. A. Pottle and F. Brady, eds., *Boswell: On Grand Tour* (New York: McGraw-Hill, 1955).

28. Lambert, *Grand Tour*, 30.

29. C. Owens, *The Grand Days of Travel* (Exeter, England: Webb and Bower Publishers, 1979), 59.

30. Greene, *Journey without Maps*, 9–10.

31. M. Dye, "Biking through Bali," *San Francisco Examiner*, 24 July 1988, Travel Section.

32. Quoted in J. Brooke, "Brazil's Forest in the Balance," *The New York Times*, 19 May 1991, Travel Section.

4. Pushing into the Periphery

1. A history of the Gurkha soldiers can be found in B. Farwell, *The Gurkhas* (New York and London: W. W. Norton and Company, 1984).

2. The critical study of myth and mythmaking can be found in Vladimir Propp, *Morphology of the Folktale*, trans. Lawrence Scott (Austin: University of Texas Press, 1968); and Claude Lévi-Strauss, "The Structural Study of Myth," *Journal of American Folklore* 68 (1955). See also the seminal works of Joseph Campbell, *The Hero with a Thousand Faces* (New York: Pantheon Books, 1949), *Creative Mythology* (New York: Viking Penguin, 1968), and *Myths, Dreams and Religion* (Dallas: Spring Publications, 1970).

3. J. R. R. Tolkien, *The Hobbit* (Boston: Houghton Mifflin, 1966), and *The Lord of the Rings*, 3 vols. (New York: Ballantine Books, 1965). For an analysis of the structure of Tolkien's work, see Anne C. Petty, *One Ring to Bind Them All: Tolkien's Mythology* (University, Ala.: University of Alabama Press, 1979).

4. Quoted from the *1993 Wilderness Travel Catalog* (Wilderness Travel, 801 Allston Way, Berkeley, CA 94710), 5.

5. Quoted from "The Art of Adventure Travel," Director Steve Conlon's letter in the 1990–1991 catalog of the Above the Clouds Trekking Agency (P.O. Box 398, Worcester, MA 01602), 2.

6. J. Jakle, *The Tourist: Travel in Twentieth-Century North America* (Lincoln: University of Nebraska Press, 1985), 27–29.

7. A. Masterton, "Cultural Tourism: Pitfalls and Possibilities," *Tour and Travel News*, 30 November 1963.

8. Alastair Reid, *Passwords: Places, Poems, Preoccupations* (Boston: Little, Brown and Company, 1963), 185–186.

9. Henri Baudet, *Paradise on Earth: Some Thoughts on European Images of Non-European Man* (New Haven: Yale University Press, 1965); Gustave Flaubert, *Intimate Notebook, 1840–1841,* trans. Francis Steegmuller (Garden City, N.Y.: Doubleday, 1967). See also Robert Arnot, *The Complete Works of Gustave Flaubert* (New York and London: M. W. Dunne, 1904); D. H. Lawrence, *Sea and Sardinia* (New York: Robert McBride and Company, 1931); D. H. Lawrence, *The Plumed Serpent* (New York: Knopf, 1951). For a critical review of the travel literature genres, see D. Porter, *Haunted Journeys: Desire and Transgression in European Travel Writing* (Princeton, N.J.: Princeton University Press, 1991).

10. Stan Stevens, "Sacred and Profaned Himalayas," *Natural History* 1:27–34 (1988): 34.

11. Gary Snyder, *The Practice of the Wild* (San Francisco: North Point Press, 1990), 81.

12. D. Meinig, "The Beholding Eye," in *The Interpretation of Ordinary Landscapes,* ed. D. Meinig (New York: Oxford University Press, 1979).

13. Snyder, *The Practice of the Wild,* 93–94.

14. J. Morris, "The Rarefied Romance of Oaxaca," *National Geographic Traveler* (1988): 67.

15. Lynn Stephen, *Zapotec Women* (Austin: University of Texas Press, 1991), 133.

16. M. Hough, *Out of Place: Restoring Identity to the Regional Landscape* (New Haven and London: Yale University Press, 1990).

17. Robert Sack, *Place, Modernity, and the Consumer's World* (Baltimore and London: Johns Hopkins University Press, 1992), 157.

18. *1993 Wilderness Travel Catalog* (Wilderness Travel, 801 Allston Way, Berkeley, CA 94710), 18.

19. Phil Dearden, "Tourism in Developing Societies: Some Observations on Trekking in the Highlands of Northern Thailand," in *Tourism: A Vital Force for Peace,* ed. Louis J. D'Amore and Jafar Jafari (Vancouver: University of Vancouver Press, 1988).

20. Ira Silver, "Marketing Authenticity in Third World Countries," *Annals of Tourism Research* 20/2 (1993): 301–318.

21. Snyder, *The Practice of the Wild,* 24.

22. Umberto Eco, *Travels in Hyperreality* (San Diego: Harcourt Brace Jovanovich, 1986), 16.

23. For discussions of place images, "sightseeing," and visual authenticity, see J. Jakle, *The Visual Elements of Landscape* (Amherst: University of Massachusetts Press, 1987); J. Appleton, *The Experience of Landscape* (London: Wiley, 1975); and Yi Fu Tuan, *Topophilia* (Englewood Cliffs, N.J.: Prentice-Hall, 1974).

24. R. Sack, *Place, Modernity, and the Consumer's World* (Baltimore: Johns Hopkins University Press, 1992), 157.

25. Susan Sontag, *On Photography* (New York: Farrar, Straus, and Giroux, 1978), 179.

26. *1993 Wilderness Travel Catalog*. Client comments on: East African Wildlife Safari, Ultimate Primate Safari, The Great Pyrennes Traverse (Wilderness Travel, 801 Allston Way, Berkeley, CA 94710), 15, 19, 37.

27. Daniel Boorstin, *The Image: A Guide to Pseudo Events in America* (New York: Harper and Row, Publishers, 1961), 78.

28. *Nepal: Urban Development Assessment* (United States Agency for International Development, Kathmandu, Nepal, and Washington, D.C., 1987), 125–130.

29. *1993 Wilderness Travel Catalog*, 52.

30. *InnerAsia Expeditions, 1990 Catalog* (InnerAsia Expeditions, 2627 Lombard Street, San Francisco, CA 94123), 28.

31. *Above the Clouds Trekking, 1989–1991* (Above the Clouds Trekking, P.O. Box 398, Worcester, MA 01602-0398).

32. *Environs, 1989–1990* (newsletter of International Expeditions, Inc., 1776 Independence Court, Birmingham, AL 35216), 48.

5. Consequences of Discovery

1. Very little has been written about Tokelau. Baseline information is provided in a document prepared for the 1992 United Nations Conference on Environment and Development (UNCED) in Brazil. See: 1991, Tokelau Country Report for UNCED.

2. Valene Smith, *Hosts and Guests: The Anthropology of Tourism* (Philadelphia: University of Pennsylvania Press, 1977).

3. E. de Kadt, *Tourism: Passport to Development?* (Oxford: Oxford University Press, 1979).

4. Marshall Berman, *All That Is Solid Melts into Air: The Experience of Modernity* (New York: Simon and Schuster, 1982), 133.

5. Gary Snyder, *The Practice of the Wild* (San Francisco: North Point Press, 1990), 82.

6. Paul Bowles, *The Sheltering Sky* (New York: New Directions Publishing Corp., 1948), 13–14.

7. John Blower, "National Parks for Developing Countries," in *National Parks, Conservation and Development: The Role of Protected Areas in Sustaining Society,* ed. J. A. McNeely and K. R. Miller (Washington, D.C.: Smithsonian Institution Press, 1984), 722–727.

8. *1993 Wilderness Travel Catalog* (Wilderness Travel, 801 Allston Way, Berkeley, CA 94710), 67.

Index

Index

Index

Oaxaca, 81; description of, 146–150; tourism in, 110–111

Opium, 99, 103–104

Orient, 39, 55; artistic representation of, 55; image of, 40

Overland road, 35, 44, 50, 68; description of, 48, 55

Oxus River, 37

Pacific, 170, 174; beaches, 25; tourism destination, 22

Pakistan, 37, 43, 60; and overland road, 69

Peace Corps, 83

Peacock Throne, 62, 74

Photography, 102; as visual consumption, 159–161

Picturesque: loss of, 43; as tourism resource, 41

Place, 2, 75, 169, 177; commercial creation of, 30, 92, 146, 162–166; conception of, 82, 143; pseudo-, 96, 161; and tourism, 10; transformation of, 3, 14, 81, 108

Polo, Marco, 45

Polynesia, 171; mariners of, 25

Polynesian Cultural Center, 85–86

Pratt, Mary Louise, 44

Rain forest, 9, 84; ecotourism in, 123

Rajasthan, 4, 81, 167–168

Rajendra, C., 15

Recreation, 6, 54

Red Fort, 73–74

Reid, Alastair, 141

Resorts, 6–7; enclave, 21

Richter, Linda, 10, 70

Rwanda, 26, 114, 121, 152

Sack, Robert, 150

Sacrifice, 71, 77

Safari, 5, 10

Said, Edward, 40–41

Samarkand, 11

Saurha, 32–33, 35

Sex tourism, 102–103

Shambala, 55

Shangri La, 55

Shifting cultivation: description of, 101

Siam, 98

Silk route, 39, 45; commerce, 65

Silver, Ira, 157

Smith, Valene, 177

Snyder, Gary, 144, 145, 179

Sontag, Susan, 160

Space: cartesian, 40; philosophical discussions of, 63, 91, 143; and time, 92; tourism, 54

Stephen, Lynn, 149

Stevenson, Robert Louis, 25

Sukothai, 98–99

Sustainable development: and adventure tourism, 108, 181; and tourism, 14–16

Taj Mahal, 74

Tamerlane, 42

Taxila, 45, 69

Tehran, 62–63

Terrae incognitae, 50

Thailand, 6, 15; ethnic groups in, 16; northern areas of, 15–16, 181; tourism development in, 16; trekking in, 96–106

Thamel, 78

Theme parks, 3, 6, 85, 139–140

Theroux, Paul, 25

Third world, 15, 19, 21; adventure tourism in, 83–85, 95, 108; national park development in, 184–185; spatial divisions of, 137–138; theo-